EMBRACED BY THE LIGHT
AND THE BIBLE

Embraced
By The Light
and the Bible

Betty Eadie and Near-Death
Experiences in the Light
of Scripture

RICHARD ABANES

HORIZON BOOKS
CAMP HILL, PENNSYLVANIA

Horizon Books
3825 Hartzdale Drive
Camp Hill, PA 17011

ISBN: 0-88965-111-6
LOC Catalog Card Number: 94-69036
© 1994 by Horizon Books
All rights reserved
Printed in the United States of America

94 95 96 97 98   5   4   3   2   1

Cover design by Robert A. Baddorf
Photo by Steve Miller

Dedication

To my beautiful wife, Bri. You are an insightful and godly woman. Thanks for keeping my papers neat, my pens capped and my spirits high. Thanks also for putting up with more dusty books and magazines than our 525-square-foot apartment was ever designed to hold. You're the best and I love you lots.

Table of Contents

Acknowledgments

This project never would have been completed without the help and encouragement of several people. My deepest appreciation goes to K. Neill Foster, Executive Vice-President/Publisher of Christian Publications, Inc., who had faith in my writing abilities despite his unfamiliarity with much of my work.

I am also grateful to my editor David Fessenden and the rest of the staff at Christian Publications. They worked very hard to get this book out on schedule.

Additional thanks must go to Bob and Gretchen Passantino (Answers in Action). They have taught me through both their words and deeds that a Christian does not have to crucify the mind in addition to the flesh in order to live a godly life.

A special note of gratitude belongs to the Christian Research Institute (CRI), which allowed my use of the Institute's library, research files and computer system.

I am especially indebted to CRI's International Coordinator, Paul Carden. He not only kept newspapers, magazines and books flowing in my direction, but also made his personal computer available to me when mid-way through the project my Powerbook 180 had its own near-death experience.

Two more individuals deserve mention: Rolly Devore, who copied important audio and video tapes for me; and my good friend Richard Perez, who often supplied lunch when I had neither the time, the energy, nor the money to get food for myself.

"Speaking the truth in love" (Ephesians 4:15) is an exhausting and difficult task, but it becomes a lot easier when there are co-laborers willing to lend a helping hand.

Foreword

In 1975, Raymond Moody introduced me and much of the world to the near-death experience (NDE) through his now classic *Life After Life*. NDEs have since been described, analyzed and discussed in countless publications. None of these post-Moody works, however, has achieved the popularity currently enjoyed by Betty Eadie's 1992 phenomenal best seller *Embraced By The Light*.

Eadie opens her book with an ostensibly straightforward dedication: "To the Light, my Lord and Savior Jesus Christ, to whom I owe all that I have. He is the 'staff' that I lean on; without him I would fall." She then proceeds to make over 150 separate references to "Jesus Christ," "Lord," "Savior," "Jesus," "Christ," "God," "Father" and "Creator."

Although Eadie identifies herself as a Christian, she freely reinterprets major tenets of Christianity according to revelations gleaned from her NDE. The scope of Eadie's modifications to Jesus' teachings is vast, yet there has been little challenge to her doctrines. Instead, Christian bookstores have actually been promoting *Embraced By The Light*. Churches and hospital chaplains are even conducting seminars based on its contents.

Melvin Morse, veteran NDE researcher and author, proclaims in his foreword to Eadie's book: "I learned more about near-death experiences from reading *Embraced By The Light* than from any other experience in my life. . . . There is a great secret contained in *Embraced By The Light*. . . . It has the power to change your life."

Richard Abanes is the first to delve into Betty Eadie's "great secret." Her message is carefully examined in the light of Scripture and compared to Mormon, Christian and New Age beliefs. Her NDE-based theology is further explored through recorded interviews with prominent NDE researchers. Abanes also provides striking insights into the making of Eadie's American bestseller by using information he obtained during taped conversations with her and her advertising agency.

As with any book dealing with religious issues, the author's point of view is key. Richard is a Christian who believes in the authority of Scripture and the deity of Jesus Christ. While reflecting these beliefs, he nonetheless relies heavily on the corroborating testimony of Eadie and others to support his arguments.

This book addresses what remains the most important issue after nearly a quarter of a century of research into the NDE—its spiritual and religious meaning.

Michael B. Sabom, M.D.
Cofounder and former vice-president of the International Association for Near-Death Studies and author of *Recollections of Death: A Medical Investigation*

Introduction

I was going through a really tough time when I read her book, and it reached inside and gave me hope.

—anonymous reader of *Embraced By The Light*[1]

On the morning of November 20, 1973, not a single *Register Star*, *Daily Post*, *City Times*, or *Tribune-Herald* mentioned the wondrous event that reportedly transpired during the previous night in Seattle, Washington's Riverton Hospital (now Highline Specialty Center). There, at approximately 9:30 p.m., 31-year-old Betty Jean Eadie allegedly began hemorrhaging as she lay recovering from a routine hysterectomy. The sudden flare-up of complications could not have arisen at a more inopportune time. A nurse's nightshift change had apparently left the suffering patient unattended in an otherwise unoccupied semi-private room. With no one by her side, Betty Eadie "died."

But the story does not end there. Eadie "returned to life" some five hours later with nearly everything she had experienced while "dead" forever locked in her memory. She supposedly came back through the portals of death with "an almost photographic view of the world beyond."[2] It is also maintained that through her spiritual journey Eadie learned the answers to some of the most thought-provoking and often-asked questions plaguing humanity: What is the meaning of life? Why is there evil and human suffering? Who is God?

After leaving the hospital, Eadie claims that she "went into a deep depression caused in part by the effects of the operation, but mainly because she found Earth was cold and unloving after experiencing the freedom of her spirit."[3] In time, however, love for her husband and children brought deliverance from the self-pity into which she had sunk. "I *had* to join life again," Eadie remembers, "[to] make myself leave the spirit world behind and move on."[4]

Thanks to the unwavering support of family and friends, Eadie started "living" again. Through their coaxing, she also began sharing her near-death experience (NDE) with others. This eventually brought her in contact with discussion groups sponsored by the Seattle chapter of the International Association for Near-Death Studies, an NDE data-gathering/support organization devoted to bringing credence to a phenomenon about which many are still skeptical.

By the late 1980s Eadie was speaking to small groups in libraries and churches. One thing led to another, and like a dream come true, Eadie's experience ended up being put in book form by a tiny publishing house called Gold Leaf Press. Her life would never be the same.

November of 1992 saw the supernatural saga released as *Embraced By The Light*. Its first printing of 20,000 copies sold out in 10 days.[5] Its second printing of 30,000 copies was snatched up just as fast.[6] Successive printings drew a similar response and suddenly, waiting lists to get a copy of the spiritual adventure had become an ever-present dilemma—Betty Eadie mania had struck.

Six months after being introduced to the public, *Embraced By The Light* hit the *New York Times* bestseller list and that was only the beginning:

- May of 1993—Bantam paid $1.5 million for paperback rights to the story (a record for a first-time author) and audio rights were auctioned off for $100,000.
- July of 1994—*Embraced By The Light* staggers onlookers by passing the two million-copies-sold mark, which in total sales, translated into more than $17 million.
- September 11, 1994—Seventy weeks after first landing on the *New York Times* bestseller list, Eadie's 147-page life-after-death narrative was still sitting in the #1 non-fiction slot—outlasting such literary megastars as Rush Limbaugh and Howard Stern.

Betty Eadie, as one television news journalist observes, has become wealthy.[7] She has also become a much sought-after speaker due to countless radio interviews, newspaper articles and a nationwide series of lectures posting ticket prices as high as $15 in advance and $17 at the door.[8] Television has been kind to Eadie as well. The syndicated news program "American Journal" and ABC's "20/20" have done extended segments on her. She has been a guest on "The Sally Jessy Raphael Show" and "The Oprah Winfrey Show." It all adds up to "almost unheard of success for a first time author."[9] Joe Eadie, Betty's husband, calls it a miracle.[10]

What is the attraction? The 52-year-old grandmother of eight says, "people are finding a lot of hope, and they are learning to use what I've written from the experience to modify their lives. . . . It has helped them overcome a lot of grief that they've suffered from the loss of their loved ones."[11]

Demand for Eadie's story may also stem from its uniqueness. Unlike similar works, *Embraced By The Light* is packed with incredible detail. Kimberly Clark-Sharp, President of the Seattle chapter of the International Association for Near–Death Studies states: "Even after interviewing over one thousand Near–Death Experiencers, Betty Eadie's account remains the most detailed and spellbinding Near–Death Experience I have ever heard."[12] Well-known NDE researcher Raymond Moody has labeled *Embraced By The Light* "the most profound and complete near-death experience ever."[13]

According to Gold Leaf Press publicity material, Eadie recalls "every detail of her spiritual ascent from a lifeless body, her last look at her family, her departure from earth into a black void, and then her journey through a tunnel towards an intense light that was filled with love."[14] She also remembers being "escorted through Heaven, a place with perfectly designed buildings that are occupied by beautiful 'beings' composed of similar but different light. . . . prayers being offered to Heaven, experienced a life-review, and much, much more."[15]

Even Christians are standing in line for the diary-like account of Eadie's voyage beyond the grave. As far back as December of 1993, *Bookstore Journal* reported that the

Berean Bookstore in Phoenix, Arizona had received "more than 80 requests for it."[16] Four months after the *Bookstore Journal* piece was published, the *National & International Religion Report* (NIRR) stated that "Christian bookstores were being bombarded with requests for a new book entitled *Embraced by the Light*."[17] A similar news article appeared in the July 1994 issue of *Charisma & Christian Life* magazine. Its subtitle read: "Betty Eadie's account of her near-death experience is in demand in Christian bookstores."[18]

In response to customer requests, Christian bookstores all over the country are ordering case after case of *Embraced By The Light*. Amy Bean, accounts representative for Gold Leaf Press, notes that "many" of the two-million-plus copies of the book that are in circulation, have been sold "through Christian bookstores."[19]

Evangelicals, charismatics and Pentecostals are being drawn to *Embraced By The Light* because the media has, on more than one occasion, referred to its author as a "devout Christian."[20] Eadie herself boldly proclaims Jesus as Lord and Savior, stating that much of what she learned in the spirit world came directly from Christ Himself. Jesus, according to Eadie, was the very "Light" who welcomed her into eternity. The book is even dedicated to "The Light, my Lord and Savior Jesus Christ. . . ."[21]

Betty Eadie is a member in good standing of the Church of Jesus Christ of Latter-day Saints (LDS)—in other words, a Mormon. Few know about her religious affiliation, however, because she and her publishing company—along with her publicist and advertising agency—have made a concerted effort to keep that information quiet, as we shall see later. Except, of course, in Utah, which is 77 percent Mormon.[22]

A *Salt Lake Tribune* book review of December 20, 1992, observed that *Embraced By The Light* public-relations material circulated in Utah prior to Eadie's publicity tour of that state advertised her as a "convert to the LDS church."[23] According to Dan Miller, Eadie's Mormon Bishop in Seattle, Washington, Eadie and her family have been attending his Ninth Ward congregation for the past 15 years.[24]

This would explain an Ogden *Standard–Examiner* article of March 6, 1993 which quotes Eadie as having said that during her "dying" experience she was told "the LDS church is 'the truest Church on the earth.' "[25]

During my interview with Eadie in January of 1994, however, she responded differently when asked which church was the truest church:

> [I]f I were to tell them [people] . . . the church that I find most rewarding, most fulfilling for me, they might not find that at all. In fact, I might be misguiding them from what they need to find for themselves.[26]

Throughout our recorded conversation, Eadie repeatedly refused to acknowledge a connection with the Latter-day Saints. Even when confronted with a statement I had obtained from Don LaFevre (Manager of Print Media Response for the LDS church) confirming that she was an active Mormon, Eadie remained elusive:

> *ABANES* I was speaking with a gentleman who is from the Public Affairs Office of the Church of Jesus Christ of Latter-day Saints and he informed me that you were an active member in good standing of the church. I understand you were inactive at the time [of your experience], but afterwards you became an active member of the church once again. Was that a result of the things that you learned from Jesus during your near-death experience?
> *EADIE* Well, in the first place I think it's rather ah, pretty much of an assumption because, ah, I don't divulge my religious beliefs—the churches that I attend now at all. And the reason for that is, some people have contacted me and said that they would join any church that I belong to. And that is not why I wrote the book. The book was written about an experience that was *generic*, as far as I am concerned . . . . I think there's a lot of guesstimate out there. . . . Not that it's a big, deep, dark secret, you understand.
> *ABANES* I've seen it in print *several* places that you are a member of the Church of Jesus Christ of Latter-day Saints.

EADIE Yeah, I've heard that too. And I've also heard that I'm Muslim, and there's another one.

ABANES I talked to this gentleman from the First President's Office in Utah, in Salt Lake. He told me that you were an active member.

EADIE Well, who *is* this gentleman?

ABANES His name was Don LaFevre, and he's with the Public Affairs Office of the First Presidency's Office in Utah, in Salt Lake.

EADIE What is the First Presidency?

The First Presidency is a "quorum made up of the President of the Church and his counselors."[27] Men in this quorum hold the most revered positions in the LDS church. It would be nearly impossible for a Mormon of 15 years not to know about the First Presidency. As Mormon apostle Bruce R. McConkie writes: "There is not any person belonging to the church who is exempt from this council of the church (D. & C. 107:80–81.)."[28]

When I attempted to pressure Eadie into admitting that she was a Mormon, she remained evasive:

ABANES He [LaFevre] is a representative of the Church of Jesus Christ of Latter-day Saints in the Public Affairs Department in Salt Lake City. He *did* confirm to me that you are indeed an active member of the Church.

EADIE How does he *know*? Where does he get that? Why does he think that?

Why would Eadie—who belongs to a movement that prides itself on the phrase "every member a missionary"— first make her LDS membership known to prospective buyers, then all but deny it? Is there a commercial motive?

Recent nationwide surveys conducted by the Barna Research Group reveal that only 6 percent of those questioned think of the LDS church "very favorably" while 19 percent polled view it "very unfavorably."[29] The *Barna Report: 1992–93* further notes that Mormonism is "least favored" by upper-income adults, born-again Christians and Bible readers.[30] Such findings indicate that Eadie's LDS identity,

18

though a marketing plus in the predominantly Mormon "Intermountain West" region where the book was first released, would very likely have cut into her sales to the general public.

Dick Baer, founder and director of Ex-Mormons and Christian Alliance of Orangevale, California cites another possible motive for Eadie's secrecy. Baer feels that *Embraced By The Light* is a kind of Trojan Horse—a conscious attempt at indirect proselytism. He characterizes the book as "a very, very sophisticated pre-evangelism tool to get people to join the Mormon Church, because all the concepts of Mormon doctrine are laid out in the book."[31] He further believes that the bestseller was crafted to "denigrate the teachings of Christianity, especially on the subject of [Christ's] deity."[32] The danger, says Baer, is that "when the Mormon missionary comes along . . . anyone who has read this book—'click'—they fall right in."[33]

In 1992, *Embraced By The Light* was the #1 selling book in Salt Lake City[34] and continues to be used by numerous Mormon study groups because it affirms key LDS doctrines.[35] Not every Mormon, however, appreciates America's newest "non-fiction" bestseller. An article in the October 23, 1993 *Salt Lake Tribune* reveals that in a meeting with "male LDS stake leaders in Sandy [Utah] last spring, Apostle Boyd K. Packer called the book 'bunk.' "[36]

Packer's charge may have a lot to do with the many *non*-LDS doctrines also contained in *Embraced By The Light*. Tom Britton, Eadie's executive assistant, told me during a phone conversation that "Betty doesn't *only* attend the LDS church. Her membership is in that church, but that's not the *only* church she attends."[37] (Eadie herself has confirmed that she does indeed attend "more than one" church.)[38]

Although Britton refused to name the other churches frequented by Eadie, they are possibly connected to the New Age movement. A substantial portion of *Embraced By The Light* lines up with Eastern philosophy, Mind Science/New Thought beliefs and occultism—the substructure of the New Age movement. New Age expert Elliot Miller, author of *A Crash Course on the New Age Movement* (Baker), has stated that Eadie advances "an odd mixture of Christian theism and New Age/metaphysical pantheism."[39]

Many individuals feel that Eadie's book chronicles a glimpse of "the other side" from which revelational truths can be gleaned. In reality, *Embraced By The Light* is a cleverly woven tale spun with threads from Mormonism, Eastern Philosophy, the Mind Sciences/New Thought and the occult.

ENDNOTES

[1] Anonymous. "20/20" program on ABC, 5/13/94.

[2] Britton, Tom. *Embraced By The Light: National Media Tour*, Gold Leaf Press Publicity Packet, p. 2.

[3] Gold Leaf Press. "What Is It Like to Die? Betty Eadie Knows," Gold Leaf Press Packet, p. 2.

[4] Eadie, Betty. *Embraced By The Light*, p. 132.

[5] Boren, Karen. *Deseret News*, "Is Death Merely the Precipice of True Birth?," 1/17/93, n.p.

[6] Perlah, Jeffrey L. *American Bookseller*, "An Amazing First-Time Success Story," June 1993, p. 64.

[7] Downs, Hugh. "20/20" program on ABC, 5/13/94.

[8] Viotti, Vicki. *The Honolulu Advertiser*, "'Embraced By The Light' Author Puts Accent on Afterlife," 6/13/94, p. B1.

[9] Downs, op. cit.

[10] Jerome, Jim. *PEOPLE*, "Heaven Can Wait," 10/11/93, p. 83.

[11] Eadie, Betty. Author's 1/25/94 interview with Eadie.

[12] Britton, op. cit., p. 1.

[13] Stuart, Janis. *Davis County Clipper*, "'Embraced' Author Nearly Squeezed Out of Auditorium," 2/12/93, p. 2.

[14] Gold Leaf Press, op. cit., p. 1.

[15] Ibid.

[16] Vixie, Linda. *Bookstore Journal*, "*Embraced By The Light*: Author is Mormon," 12/93, p. 14.

[17] n.a. *Christian Retailing*, "Best-selling Book Affirms Mormon Tenets and Teaching," 6/18/94, n.p.

[18] Ford, Marcia. *Charisma & Christian Life*, "Mormon Book Lures Christians," July 1994, p. 64.

[19] Ibid.

[20] Perlah, op. cit., cf. *The Arizona Republic*, "Visiting Death: Woman Tells of Glimpse of Paradise" by Kathie Price, 3/13/93, p. B7.

[21] Eadie, *Embraced*, p. iii.

[22] n.a. *The Evangel*, "Utah Divorce Rate Higher than Norm," Vol. XLI, No. 5, Summer edition, p. 12.

[23] Swenson, Paul. *Salt Lake Tribune*, "Utah Under Cover: Area Books & Authors," 12/20/92, p. PE 11.

[24] Miller, Dan. Author's 1/21/94 interview with Miller.

[25] Phillips, Valerie. [Ogden] *Standard-Examiner*, "Author Shares Love of Life After Death in an Embrace," 3/6/93, n.p.

[26] Eadie, author's 1/25/94 interview, op. cit.

[27] LDS Church. *Gospel Principles*, p. 353.

[28] McConkie, Bruce. *Mormon Doctrine*, p. 283.

[29] Barna, George. *The Barna Report: 1992–1993*, p. 62.

[30] Ibid., p. 64.

[31] Baer, Dick. Author's 1/25/94 interview with Baer.

[32] Ibid.

[33] Ibid.

[34] Swenson, Paul. *Salt Lake Tribune*, "Utah Undercover: Area Books & Authors," 12/20/92, p. PE-11.

[35] Stack, Peggy Fletcher. *Salt Lake Tribune*, "Mormon's Book on Afterlife Gains National Response," 10/23/93, p. D2.

[36] Ibid.

[37] Britton, Tom. Author's 1/94 interview with Britton.

[38] Eadie, author's 1/25/94 interview, op. cit

[39] Miller, Elliot. Author's 1/94 discussion with Miller.

PART 1

EMBRACED
BY
MORMONISM

[C]onvince us of our errors of doctrine, if we have any, by reason, by logical arguments, or by the Word of God, and we will be ever grateful for the information, and you will ever have the pleasing reflection that you have been instruments in the hands of God of redeeming your fellow beings from the darkness which you may see enveloping their minds.

— Orson Pratt, Mormon Apostle[1]

CHAPTER 1

Mormon Masquerade

[T]he book was meant to go out to the world, not just to LDS members.

— Betty J. Eadie[2]

Questions concerning Betty Eadie's religious affiliation began surfacing in California around December of 1993, the same month a *Bookstore Journal* article substantiated, to some degree, rumors that America's newest literary sensation was a Mormon. The brief news story, however, did not provide *solid* proof of its allegation.

The new year brought only more speculation and confusion as the secular media continued painting Eadie as a churchgoing Christian.[3] By the end of January, *Embraced By The Light* was making a serious impact on the Christian community. Consequently, I decided on January 21, 1994 to once and for all separate fact from fiction concerning Betty Eadie.

After several hours of countless phone calls to Salt Lake City, Utah and Seattle, Washington, I found myself in contact with Dan Miller, Mormon Bishop of metro Seattle's Ninth Ward. (A ward is the basic "ecclesiastical district or church unit in and through which the programs of the [LDS] Church are administered. . . .")[4]

"Betty is not a real *active* member," Miller said, "and this goes back before the book was published. . . . Her activity has been sort of lukewarm."

I asked, "Are you sure this is the same Betty Eadie?"

"Oh, yes," he replied, "I've had a lot of contact with Betty and know the family well."

Despite Eadie's nominal involvement with the church, local Latter-day Saints loved attending her pre-*Embraced By The Light* lectures about the night she "died" and met Jesus. The talks profoundly affected them because the NDE validated so many of their Mormon beliefs. One woman by the name of Jane Barfuss was so moved that she began jotting down Eadie's story. After attending three lectures, Barfuss "typed up a 16-page synopsis and sent it to friends and family in Salt Lake City who, in turn, sent copies to more friends."[5] This version of Eadie's near-death drama, entitled "Spirit World," finally found its way into the hands of Mormon book editor Curtis Taylor of Aspen Books (Murray, Utah). He, too, was profoundly moved.

"Her story hit me hard," remembers Taylor. "I was a madman for it."[6]

Taylor was in a perfect position to buy the rights to Eadie's story, but by the time he tracked her down she had already sold them to Cedar Fort, Inc. (a small regional publisher) in Springville, Utah for a mere $1,000 in advance royalties.[7] Undaunted, Taylor and some of his fellow workers at Aspen Books scraped together $50,000 to purchase the rights. What followed was nothing short of pure marketing genius.

Exit Aspen, Enter Gold Leaf

It has been widely reported, and accepted as true, that Curtis Taylor became so enthralled with Eadie's experience that after securing the rights to her story, he personally opened Gold Leaf Press in Placerville, California specifically to publish it.

Such an account—coupled with Eadie's success—has made for a dramatic, if not inspiring, tale of one man's entrepreneurship, his belief in a book and the gamble he took by starting a brand new publishing house:

> Taylor knew immediately he had a hit. He tracked down Eadie, who knew "by the spirit" the match was right. Taylor started Gold Leaf Press in California specifically to publish the book.[8]

Embraced By The Light defies virtually every precept
of modern publishing: Ms. Eadie had never written a
book before, and Gold Leaf Press had never published one.[9]

But another story—known only by a few individuals—was
recounted to me by a high-ranking officer at Stilson & Stilson, the Salt Lake City advertising agency which handled
publicity for *Embraced By The Light* during its first year of
release.

According to Stilson & Stilson, Gold Leaf was not really
started by Taylor per se. Nor was it begun specifically to
publish *Embraced By The Light*. Taylor's new press was actually formed by Aspen Books in order to publish and
market on a national scale—rather than just on a regional
level—specific works with mass appeal potential. This
means that although Gold Leaf had "technically" never published, those running it had published many times and knew
exactly what they were doing. It also appears that *Embraced
By The Light* was simply the first book to have access to the
broader market via Gold Leaf Press,[10] which is actually
owned by Aspen.[11]

But why would an established publishing house need to
market books on a national scale under another imprint?
The answer may have a lot to do with the fact that Aspen
Books is an LDS owned and operated press which carries
strictly Mormon titles.[12] Aspen may have thought it contrary
to market savvy to release nationally-targeted books from
the same publishing house producing such titles as *The LDS
Speaker's Sourcebook*, and *Offenders for a Word: How Anti-
Mormons Play Word Games to Attack Latter-day Saints*.[13]

Aspen's choice of where to locate their new publishing
firm also suggests an awareness of how non-Mormons view
Mormonism—the predominantly Mormon state of Utah was
left behind in favor of Placerville, California. Perhaps Aspen
felt that a new press located in the far west state would raise
fewer questions from the general public than one located in
the heart of Mormon country.

But when it came time to release *Embraced By The Light* in
November of 1992, Aspen/Gold Leaf wisely returned to the
LDS stronghold of Salt Lake City, Utah to launch the book's

first 20,000 copies.[14] Just prior to this, Taylor enlisted the help of Stilson & Stilson, a "very low-profile" advertising agency with clientele ranging from traditional retail stores to Larry Miller, owner of the Utah Jazz basketball team.[15]

Bill Kittel, vice-president of Stilson & Stilson, maintains that his organization does more book-publishing advertising than any other agency he knows of in Utah, and maybe in the entire country. "We're a little different than most agencies," he says, "in that our primary focus on any of the projects that we get into is research oriented."[16]

In other words, rather than being just an ordinary, run-of-the-mill advertising/publicity agency, Stilson & Stilson does research that enables them to get a particular product sold to a particular segment of the population. They did an outstanding job with *Embraced By The Light*.

My Fellow Mormons . . .

Eadie's Mormon faith was practically shouted from the housetops when her book was first released. For example, at the suggestion of Stilson & Stilson, Gold Leaf inserted into each book a one-page flyer entitled "Of Special Interest to Members of The Church of Jesus Christ of Latter-day Saints" (see photo section).

It tells of Eadie's conversion through the evangelistic efforts of two Mormon missionaries in San Antonio, Texas. The insert additionally speaks of how Eadie, after her near-death experience, began to seriously study the doctrines of the LDS Church only to be "continually surprised at how accurately the [Mormon] gospel reflected what she had seen."[17]

The six-paragraph message further indicates that Eadie is anything but a "lukewarm" Mormon. "After her death experience," it reads, "she and her family became active in the Church. She has served since in various auxiliaries, including in the Primary [an association through which young children receive special guidance, teaching, and social experience] and Ward Young Woman's president."[18]

The flyer also reveals Eadie's status as a "Temple Mormon," a coveted LDS position reserved only for members who have been given a Temple Recommendation from Mormon leadership. This certificate is issued only to those who have diligently served in the LDS Church and have been obedient to the tenets of the LDS faith. It is used "to identify persons as members of the Church or to certify to their worthiness to receive certain ordinances or blessings [in LDS temples]."[19]

Early Utah sales of *Embraced By The Light* skyrocketed. Then, Stilson & Stilson came through again by arranging for Eadie to embark on a whirlwind speaking tour of Utah and its neighboring Mormon homelands of Nevada and Arizona. The LDS public was so rabid for a book supporting Mormonism that Eadie's lectures often resembled the frenzied activities of a rock concert. The following occurred when some 5,000 residents of Utah made their way to a high school in the small town of Woods Cross, located near Bountiful, Utah:

> They abandoned their cars on the grass and on the sidewalks. They crashed through the back doors. And police had to be called to control the crowds. . . . Prior to the engagement, vehicles were lined up blocking three freeway exits and entrances as they attempted to reach the school. . . . The parking lot was overflowing with vehicles and when all of the legal spaces were full, people parked illegally. . . . Almost instantly the auditorium was full, then the gym was full, and then the Little Theatre was full. . . . "People on the inside were opening secured doors to let others in . . . ."[20]

> [There were] several two-car accidents involving people on their way to hear Eadie. . . . Another woman lost control of her vehicle and shot off the road trying to avoid a collision with another vehicle. In the city traffic was even worse. Cars were at a standstill and there was no place to park. You couldn't move. . . .[21]

There's an old saying that goes: "If it ain't broke, don't fix it." Given Eadie's early successes, one would think that Gold Leaf had found a marketing motto in this much-used phrase, especially after the Woods Cross episode. But when it came time to offer *Embraced By The Light* to the non-Mormon public, the California-based publisher along with their ad agency chose a different philosophy—be a chameleon.

You Can Please Everyone

Something very significant was missing from the copies of *Embraced By The Light* that went out to non-Mormon states—the flyer that had been inserted into the first several thousand books.

Distinctively Mormon words and phrases were absent from the newly printed books as well. These had been edited out and replaced with more generic language (see Appendix A). One section concerning abortion (which Mormons staunchly oppose) was markedly softened, in an apparent effort to not be offensive to those who are pro-abortion.

The most drastic change in marketing came in the form of an uncharacteristic silence by Eadie about being a Mormon. The 15-year Mormon was suddenly saying that she did not want to divulge her denomination because she did not "want the sharing of her experience to be confused with proselytizing."[22]

Without a Mormon label, Eadie's book started being picked up by everybody from atheists to occultists. Then, when she began calling herself a devout Christian, her main audience quickly became the Christian community. "[Christians are] finding it and spreading the word," Eadie told one reporter.[23]

No one seemed at all curious about Eadie's religious background. When I was finally able to ask her during our interview why she would not divulge her denomination, she responded predictably: "The book is never meant to proselytize. . . . It was never meant for a particular church."[24]

Just a few months earlier, however, in an interview with the *Salt Lake Tribune*, Eadie had spoken quite openly about her religious affiliation. She even mentioned plans to write another book responding to the questions that had been collected from the "many [Mormon] firesides"[25] at which she had spoken. (Firesides are LDS meetings during which inspirational talks are given.)

During this same interview, Eadie openly shared about how public speaking engagements had given her the chance almost daily to bear her "testimony" (Mormon assurance that the LDS church is the true church). She also said, "It's like being at a [Mormon] testimony meeting every day."[26] (A "testimony meeting" is a monthly worship service of the LDS church during which individuals "offer extemporaneous descriptions of their beliefs.")[27]

Eadie has used her "I-don't-want-to-proselytize" response numerous times. During one interview on a Christian radio talk show, for instance, she stated:

> At the beginning, of course, I sought out a church that I felt would best suit my needs after having had this experience. I at first told people the church that I belong to. People said, "You tell me what church that you belong to; I will quickly join it." I felt that that was a wrong reason for them joining the church. And so I backed away. I have learned you are where you are because that is where you have grown and that as time goes on you too will grow and that is the natural process. But if people are comfortable where they are, far be it from me to come in and try to make that change.[28]

Such a stand directly contradicts a rather inspiring and admirable sentiment expressed in the flyer which originally appeared in the Utah-issued books. It describes Eadie's desire to bring as many people as possible into the LDS church:

> She [Eadie] says that if she could choose her neighbors, she would prefer to live near nonmembers so she could set a good example and eventually bring them into the Church.[29]

Eadie's transformation into someone worried about proselytizing was not a heartfelt conviction, according to Bill Kittel, but rather "a group decision."[30] It was, in fact, part of a marketing strategy agreed upon by Eadie, Stilson & Stilson and Gold Leaf Press:

> From a marketing standpoint we chose not to address that issue [Eadie's religious affiliation]. A lot of times if you say it's *not* LDS, or whatever, then it just makes it seem more like it is. . . . Our approach was, "Hey, this is a great story. There's a lot of interest regardless of what [the] religion [is] of the person that had it." We chose, basically, not to address it. We didn't try to *hide* the fact that she was, but we also didn't say that she was.[31]

Kittel maintains everyone involved felt that "by bringing a religious slant to it" that they would be "unable to reach a significant number of people to get the story out."[32]

Toward the end of my conversation with Kittel, he assured me that they were all thinking of it more from a " 'Hey, this story can really help people [point of view]' rather than a 'We can sell a ton of books and make a lot of money [point of view].' "[33]

Hidden agendas, secrecy and manipulation of truth may not be as foreign to Mormon practices as one might expect. In support of this allegation is a long history of Mormon controversy.

The FEN Secret

In 1988, businessmen Jared Brown and Seldon Young decided to start a for-profit corporation called the Family Entertainment Network (FEN). They formed the organization in order to produce animated films for children. One of the first series of tapes released was a 12-video set entitled "Animated Stories from the New Testament."

When the product hit video markets it was immediately praised for "its high quality animation, appealing musical score, and engaging renderings of New Testament events and parables."[34] Christians were delighted that professional-quality, animated films for children—which told the wonderful story of Jesus—had finally been created. The tapes began being purchased by the thousands, and were soon in churches and Christian homes all across America. The year 1991 saw total sales of the $350-$400 video series top $25 million.[35]

Only after more than a million copies of the tapes had been sold via nationwide television commercials, shopping mall booths, and Christian bookstores (through Spring Arbor Distributors) did everyone discover that FEN was owned and operated by Mormons. It was further realized that Mormon doctrines had crept into the videos through catchy tunes and subtle dialogue.

Numerous LDS church members had been involved in making the videos. They included: Jared Brown (FEN President), Seldon Young (co-owner), Richard Rich (animation), Orson Scott Card (screenplays), Lex de Azevedo (musical scores), Carol Lynn Pearson (lyrics) and Brigham Young University Professor Ivan Crossland (voice of Jesus).[36]

The Christian public then learned that Brown and Young were the same men who had started Living Scriptures, a Utah-based company formed in 1974 "primarily to market audio cassette dramatizations of Latter-day Saint scripture and history to Mormon customers."[37]

In a November 15, 1992 conversation with James Walker of Watchman Fellowship, Brown admitted that FEN had been set up so that Living Scriptures (producer of "Animated Stories from the Book of Mormon") could expand "into the larger Christian market."[38]

The similarities between the formation of Gold Leaf Press and the formation of FEN are noteworthy. FEN, like Gold Leaf, was based *outside* Mormon territory (i.e., in Dallas, Texas) while its parent company remained headquartered in Utah.

Also, in the same way that Utah residents received information about *Embraced By The Light* that was elsewhere denied, information about FEN products eluded many. Some non-Mormons were actually told by FEN spokespersons that the company had absolutely nothing to do with Mormons or the Mormon church.[39] In Utah, however, the truth about FEN was proudly publicized. The following classified advertisement appeared in an Orem, Utah newspaper of February 17, 1988:

REPRESENT THE BEST OF ANIMATED VIDEO!
The animated Book of Mormon is a phenomenal success, but now with "THE KING IS BORN" [an FEN title], the animated video of the Christmas story, the available Christian market is over 100 times as large as the market that Living Scriptures has served.[40]

Brown and Young were eventually pressured into revising their videos based on recommendations given to them by evangelicals from various counter-cult ministries. But since Mormons are required to give 10 percent of their gross income to the LDS church,[41] Christians, through supporting a Mormon-owned and operated business, had indirectly contributed a very large amount of cash to a religious empire already spending an estimated $4.7 billion dollars a year to further its goals.[42]

In a show of good faith, FEN offered to exchange Mormon doctrine-tainted videos for corrected tapes—all Christians had to do was pay a $4 shipping charge.[43]

Dunn's Deceptions

Taking a detour around truth can occasionally backfire. Such was the case for Paul H. Dunn, a well-respected Mormon apostle, popular teacher, author and role model.[44] For years Dunn had illustrated the great "truths" of Mormonism through stories taken from his own life.

There was the tale about how his best friend "died in his arms during a World War II battle, while imploring Dunn to teach America's youth about patriotism."[45]

Then there was the riveting account of "how God protected him as enemy machine-gun bullets ripped away his clothing, gear and helmet without ever touching his skin."[46]

Another inspirational yarn explained "how perseverance and Mormon values led him to play major-league baseball for the St. Louis Cardinals."[47]

Unfortunately, none of Dunn's stories were true: his "dead" friend was alive; only the heel of Dunn's boot was touched by a bullet; and he never played for the Cardinals. Dunn admitted his exaggerations when confronted by the media, but defended his actions, saying that the fabrications were necessary "to illustrate his theological and moral points."[48]

For the sake of teaching his "moral points," Dunn had apparently found it necessary to ignore the Mormon Church's 13th article of faith: "We believe in being honest. . . ."[49] A February 16, 1991 article that appeared in *The Arizona Republic* lists several of Dunn's many tall tales:

> [He was] . . . the sole survivor among 11 infantrymen in a 100-yard race against death, during which one burst of machine-gun fire ripped his right boot off, another tore off his ammunition and canteen belt and yet another split his helmet in half—all without wounding him.
>
> [He kept] . . . a Japanese prisoner from being butchered by GIs bent on revenge for the torture-slayings of American soldiers.
>
> [He wrestled] . . . a dynamite pack off a child kamikaze infiltrator, saving himself and the child.
>
> [He] . . . survived being run over by an enemy tank, while others were crushed.
>
> [He was] . . . one of only six in his 1,000-man combat group who survived, and was the only one of the six who wasn't wounded.[50]

Dunn's lies were discovered by Lynn Packer, a Brigham Young University (BYU) teacher and free-lance writer who, after notifying BYU leaders of the information, was told to "permit church leaders to deal privately with the Dunn matter."[51] In a September 30, 1987 memo, Packer's BYU department chairman, Gordon Whiting, told him:

> After providing the information, we accept the judgment of those responsible. We will not take accusations against a General Authority to the media. . . . [publication of such material] will damage the church, will damage the university, and will damage you.[52]

That same night Packer was reportedly offered a deal: "[D]on't publish the story and you can teach at BYU as long as you want."[53] Packer claims that his immediate superiors in the church, elders James E. Faust and David B. Haight, knew about the arrangement and did nothing. Packer's integrity motivated him to ignore the warning and take the information to *The Arizona Republic*. The move cost him his BYU position.

What about Dunn? He was placed on early "retirement" and eventually issued a public apology in which he stated, "I confess that I have not always been accurate in my public talks and writings."[54] Despite the events surrounding his so-called "retirement," Dunn continues to be "a popular public speaker and the most prolific author among current and former church leaders. He receives royalties from 23 inspirational cassette tapes and 28 books, many of which contain his war and baseball stories."[55]

Why Pick on Mormons?

LDS fraud and deception leads all the way back to Joseph Smith, the founder of Mormonism. A December 1990 *Sunstone* magazine article entitled "History of LDS Fraud Chronicled" listed several examples.[56] The following represents only some of the more notable cases:

> **1836:** Joseph Smith and other prominent Mormon leaders start the Kirtland Safety Society Bank and issue bogus money that they will not redeem "for equal value in silver or gold. . . . Joseph Smith and a cashier are accused of embezzlement."
>
> **1844:** "The *Nauvoo Expositor* [newspaper] accuses Joseph Smith of selling land at inflated prices. [Joseph Smith declares the *Expositor* a public nuisance and has it destroyed . . . .]."
>
> **1890s:** The Utah Loan and Trust Company, headed by high-ranking Mormon apostles (including Joseph F. Smith, sixth President of the church–1901) becomes insolvent. In the bank's dubious position, "all board members could be indicted on felony charges . . . . Elder Grant convinces Provo miner magnate

Jesse Knight to put up $10,000 to rescue the bank from financial troubles."

1925: The brother of high-level LDS Apostle George A. Smith (eighth president of the church–1945) becomes the founding director of an enterprise to sell burial plots. "By 1932, the company is in receivership and the company principals are charged with fraud . . . . Apostle Smith pulls strings in all arenas to have the charges dropped. . . . The men are acquitted, but the court determines that fraudulent representations were made."

1990s: "Carl W. Martin and Michael D. Wright, both prominent Mormons, have pleaded guilty to non-related penny stock swindles in the past several months. One stock broker who specializes in identifying and exploiting bogus penny stock schemes says the Utah market is the 'slimiest financial market in the U.S., bar none.' "

By citing the above instances of fraud, I do not mean to say that *all* Mormons are dishonest. I am personally acquainted with Latter-day Saints who are honest, hard-working individuals with a high degree of integrity. I only raise these issues to show that there is a disturbing amount of deception occurring among a group of people who—according to their leadership—are morally and ethically superior.

Brigham Young, the LDS church's second President, stated, "This people [Mormons] are the best people that ever lived upon the earth."[57]

Joseph Fielding Smith, 10th president of the Mormon Church, writes: "SAINTS ARE THE BEST PEOPLE. *We are, notwithstanding our weaknesses, the best people in the world . . . . this truth is evident to all who are willing to observe for themselves. We are morally clean, in every way equal, and in many ways superior to any other people"*(emphasis added).[58]

Mormons view themselves not only as *morally* and *ethically* superior, but also *spiritually* superior. They believe, for example, that their church is "the only true and living church upon the face of the whole earth"[59] and that " 'the power of God unto salvation' (Rom. 1:16) is absent from all but the Church of Jesus Christ of Latter-day Saints . . . ."[60]

According to LDS apostle Bruce McConkie, the Mormon church is "the only organization authorized by the Almighty to preach his gospel and administer the ordinances of salvation, the only Church which has power to save . . . ."[61]

Mormons take this high-minded view of their church because they feel that although Christian denominations have the bare essentials of the gospel (i.e., belief that there is a God, knowledge of Jesus Christ, the concept of salvation through Christ's death, etc.), Mormonism alone possesses "the fullness" of the gospel.[62]

This "fullness," says McConkie, "was restored to earth in the last days through the instrumentality of Joseph Smith. It is found only in The Church of Jesus Christ of Latter-day Saints."[63] The LDS gospel includes, but is not limited to: 1) the belief that we are all *literally* sons and daughters of God the Father; 2) the concept that all of us existed before we were born; and 3) the view that Jesus Christ and God the Father are two separate gods.

All of these doctrines are promoted to varying degrees in *Embraced By The Light*. On page 46, Eadie even makes a subtle reference to Mormonism when she writes: "There *is* a fullness of the gospel, but most people will not attain it here."[64]

In 1954, the Mormon church's 10th president wrote: "The Latter-day Saints are the only people in the world, as far as my knowledge goes, who have a clear, distinct doctrine in regard to the questions: Where did we come from? Why are we here? and, Where are we going?"[65]

Thanks to *Embraced By The Light*, Smith's comment is now obsolete. Millions have "embraced" Mormonism—without even realizing it.

ENDNOTES

[1] Pratt, Orson. *The Seer*, "Celestial Marriage," July 12, 1843, pp. 15–16.

[2] Phillips, Valerie. [Ogden] *Standard-Examiner*, "Author Shares Love of Life After Death in an Embrace," 3/6/93, n.p.

[3] Price, Kathie. *The Arizona Republic*, "Visiting Death: Woman Tells of Glimpse of Paradise," 3/13/93, p. B7.

[4] McConkie, Bruce. *Mormon Doctrine*, p. 827.

[5] Jerome, Jim. PEOPLE, "Heaven Can Wait," 10/11/93, p. 83; cf. Eadie, Betty. *Embraced By The Light*, acknowledgments.

[6] Ibid., p. 83.

[7] Perlah, Jeffrey L. *American Bookseller*, "An Amazing First-Time Success Story," June 1993, p. 64; cf. Author's 8/14/94 interview with Bill Kittel; Jerome, Jim. PEOPLE, "Heaven Can Wait," 10/11/93, p. 83.

[8] Ho, Vanessa. *Seattle Times*, "Brush with Death Puts Her in the Publishing Spotlight," 6/27/93, p. L3.

[9] Cox, Meg. *Wall Street Journal*, "Death Conquers Bestseller Lists As Boomers Age," 2/23/94, p. B1.

[10] Kittel, Bill. Author's 8/4/94 interview with Kittel.

[11] Fitzgerald, Nephi. Author's 6/28/94 telephone conversation with Fitzgerald (Aspen employee).

[12] Ibid.

[13] Aspen Books Order Form, June 1994.

[14] Boren, Karen. *Deseret News*, "Is Death Merely the Precipice of True Birth?," 1/17/93, n.p.; cf. Kittel, Bill. Author's 8/4/94 interview with Kittel.

[15] Kittel, op. cit.

[16] Ibid.

[17] Gold Leaf Press flyer. "Of Special Interest to Members of The Church of Jesus Christ of Latter-day Saints."

[18] Ibid.

[19] McConkie, op. cit., p. 620.

[20] Stuart, Janis. *Davis County Clipper*, " 'Embraced' Author Nearly Squeezed Out of Auditorium," 2/12/93, p. 2.

[21] Eddington, Mark. *Davis County Clipper*, "Eadie's Appearance Ties Up Traffic," 2/12/93, p. 2.

[22] Price, op. cit.

[23] Miller, Leslie. *USA Today*, "Betty Eadie, Shedding 'Light' on Her Visit to Heaven," 8/12/93, p. 5D.

[24] Eadie, Betty. Author's 1/25/94 interview with Eadie.

[25] Stack, Peggy Fletcher. *Salt Lake Tribune*, 10/23/93, "Mormon's Book on Afterlife Gains National Response," p. D2.

[26] Ibid.

[27] Ibid.

[28] Eadie, Betty. WMUZ 3/3/94 taped interview with Al Kresta.

[29] Gold Leaf Press flyer, op. cit.

[30] Kittel, op. cit.

[31] Ibid.

[32] Ibid.

[33] Ibid.

[34] Carden, Paul. *Christian Research Journal*, "Family Entertainment Network Moves to Dispel Controversy Over New Testament Videos," Summer 1992, p.6.

[35] Vixie, Linda. *Bookstore Journal*, "Company's Mormon Connections Raise Questions," 11/91, p. 19.

[36] Carden, op. cit.

[37] n.a. *Watchman Expositor*, "Mormon Ties to Children's Bible Videos," vol. 9 no.1, 1992, p. 1.

[38] Ibid., pp. 1–2.

[39] Hall, Tom. 4/3/91 private letter from Tom Hall to all Ex-Mormons for Jesus Ministries, p. 1.

[40] n.a. *Utah County Journal*, "Journal Classifieds," 2/17/88, p. 20.

[41] McConkie, op. cit., p. 797.

[42] n.a. *The Arizona Republic*, "Counting Its Blessings," 6/30/91, p. A1.

[43] Carden, op. cit., p. 34.

[44] Robertson, Richard. *The Arizona Republic*, "Mormon Leader Admits Exaggerating Stories," 2/16/91, p. B9.

[45] Ibid.

[46] Ibid.

[47] Ibid.

[48] Ibid.

[49] Talmage, James E. *A Study of the Articles of Faith*, p. 3.

[50] Robertson, op. cit.

[51] Anderson, Vern. *Salt Lake Tribune*, "Pursuit of Dunn Story Proves Costly for Veteran Journalist," 2/21/91, p. B3.

[52] Ibid.

[53] Ibid.

[54] n.a. *The Washington Times*, "Official Apologizes for Embellishing Stories," 10/28/91, n.p.

[55] n.a. *Salt Lake Tribune*, "Popular LDS Speaker Admits Telling Tales About War, Baseball," 2/16/91, p. 2B.

[56] n.a. *Sunstone*, December 1990, "History of LDS Fraud Chronicled," pp. 59–60.

[57] Young, Brigham. *Journal of Discourses*, 4:269, "A Discourse, by President Brigham Young, Delivered in Great Salt Lake City, March 8, 1857."

[58] Smith, Joseph Fielding. *Doctrines of Salvation*, 1:236.

[59] McConkie, op. cit., p. 136.

[60] Jackson, Kent P. *Ensign*, "Early Signs of the Apostasy," 12/84, p. 9.

[61] McConkie, op. cit.

[62] Smith, Joseph. *Pearl of Great Price*, "Joseph Smith—History 1:34."

[63] McConkie, op. cit., p. 334.

[64] Eadie, *Embraced*, p. 46.

[65] Smith, Joseph Fielding, op. cit., 1:56.

CHAPTER 2

Thank You, Joseph Smith

*If heavenly messengers . . . have visited this earth . . .
bringing messages from God, as claimed by the Prophet
Joseph Smith, then we have the most important message
that can go out to the world. . . . With this thought in
mind, we shall proceed to analyze the contribution of
these heavenly messengers. We suggest the reader assume the position of judge and jury, withholding his ver-
dict until the evidence herein presented has been fully
considered.*

— Le Grand Richards, Mormon Apostle[1]

The first three chapters of *Embraced By The Light* do not
reveal a clear link to Mormonism. Just a few pages into
chapter four, however, Eadie's doctrinal point of view emerges in a description of what occurred shortly after her al-
leged death: "[T]hree men suddenly appeared at my side
. . . . They spoke to me. They had been with me for 'eternities,' they said."[2]

The term "eternities" is often used by Mormons.[3] It can be
difficult to determine its precise meaning, however, since
Mormons themselves seem not to have a very concrete explanation for it. According to one Christian missionary to
Latter-day Saints, "The plural eternities is one that occurs
frequently in Mormonism. I have never found a good explanation of it. When I have asked Mormons about it, they

said they have never thought about it. They are surprised that I am puzzled by it since they have grown up using it."[4]

"Eternities" presumably designates the various time spans existing in the spiritual realm. Author Gilbert W. Schraffs, a staunch defender of his Mormon faith, uses it in this manner: "That is where real joy comes in this life and in the eternities."[5]

Eadie makes several references to "eternities" in *Embraced By The Light* (pp. 31, 86, 121, 122). Each has a distinctively Mormon ring. For example:

Mormonism	Embraced By The Light
You may explore all the *eternities that have been*, were it possible, then come to that which we now understand . . . (emphasis added).[6]	My memory was opened further than before, reaching back beyond the creation of our earth into *eternities past* (p. 86, emphasis added).
[T]here was a *past eternity* and there will be a *future eternity* (emphasis added).[7]	He [God] sees into our *eternal pasts and futures* . . . (p. 106, emphasis added).

Eadie's references to "eternities," or time periods in the spirit world, are directly related to the Mormon doctrine of preexistence. This doctrine is foundational to both Mormonism and Eadie's NDE. Consequently, it is the first similarity between the two we must examine.

Didn't I Know You Before We Were Born?

Mormonism teaches that everyone lived in heaven before being born on earth. In heaven, we were "reared to maturity, becoming grown spirit men and women prior to coming upon this earth."[8] One LDS apostle explains: "*Pre-existence* is the term commonly used to describe the *pre-mortal existence* of the spirit children of God the Father.[9]

This is exactly what Eadie claims to have remembered soon after dying: ". . . I began to see images in my mind of a time long ago, of an existence before my life on earth. . . . The fact of a pre-earth life crystallized in my mind . . . ."[10]

Not only did all of us exist before our births, Eadie contends, but we also had relationships with one another. In reference to the same three spirit guides who had greeted her soon after "dying," Eadie says, ". . . I knew that these were my choicest friends in that greater life and that they had chosen to be with me."[11]

How long ago does someone exist in heaven before his or her birth on earth? Apparently, as far as creation itself. In fact, Eadie says we actually helped God do the creating: "All people as spirits in the pre-mortal world took part in the creation of the earth. . . . Each spirit who was to come to earth assisted in planning the conditions on earth . . . ."[12]

Mormon leaders agree with Eadie. McConkie writes: "[H]e [Christ] was aided in the creation of this earth by 'many of the noble and great' spirit children of the Father . . . ."[13]

According to Mormon literature, "Every form of life had an existence in a spirit form before being born on this earth."[14] Eadie also asserts, "Everything was created of spirit matter before it was created physically . . . ."[15]

Of course, everyone did not initially start out as a fully formed spirit being. We originally came from eternal spirit matter (see last Eadie quote) known as "intelligence," or spirit element, which at some point was organized into heavenly spirit babies. In other words, portions of this eternal "intelligence" were formed into "intelligences."

Bruce McConkie explains that the "intelligence or spirit element became intelligences after the spirits were born as individual [spirit] entities."[16] Portions of this self-existent spirit element "are born as spirit children, or in other words, the intelligence which cannot be created or made, because it is self-existent, is organized into intelligences."[17]

Mormon terminology such as "spirit matter," "intelligence" and "intelligences" appear often in *Embraced By The Light*. On page 32, Eadie describes how, while in the company of her three previously mentioned spirit guides, she telepathically communicated feelings and thoughts to them "spirit to spirit—from intelligence to intelligence."

The significance of this statement is found in Eadie's use of the phrase "intelligence to intelligence" in conjunction with "spirit to spirit." Mormons believe that the mind is inseparable from the spirit. It is an integral part of that inner "eternal matter" used to form the soul. The LDS volume *Mormon Doctrine* reads: "Man's intelligence is in his spirit and not in the natural or mortal body. Thus we find the Prophet [Joseph Smith] speaking of 'the mind or the intelligence which man possesses' . . . 'the soul, the mind of man, the immortal spirit [i.e. the intelligence].' "[18]

It is obvious that Eadie has such a meaning in mind when she uses the word "intelligence." On pages 34–35, for example, she says, "I came to know that each of my children . . . . were individual spirits, like myself, with an intelligence that was developed before their lives on earth." She makes similar references to "intelligence" and "intelligences" on pages 55, 57, 79 and 80.

A legitimate question is: Why doesn't anyone remember being organized from spirit matter into "intelligences" and/or the subsequent life we lived in heaven? According to Eadie, everything is erased from our memories as we enter this world. "Birth is a sleep and a forgetting," she writes.[19]

This expression about birth being "a sleep and a forgetting" is truly beautiful, and well it should be—the phrase is from "Ode: Intimations of Immortality From Recollections of Early Childhood," by famous English poet William Wordsworth (1770–1850). Wordsworth wrote: "Our *birth is but a sleep and a forgetting*" (emphasis added)."[20] Eadie prefaces her poetic comment by merely saying, "Then the thought came to me, referring to us all . . . ."[21]

Whether Eadie's "thought" came to her while reading an anthology of Wordsworth poems is difficult to determine because there is always the possibility that she may have learned the phrase from *The Gospel Through the Ages*, a popular LDS book by Mormon apostle Milton R. Hunter. On page 128 of this Mormon classic, Hunter writes: "The poet Wordsworth beautifully expressed the foregoing divine doctrine when he wrote the following: Our birth is but a sleep and a forgetting."

Another popular Mormon book, *The Way to Perfection*, states essentially the same thing on page 130: "The poet Wordsworth obtained an inspirational glimpse of this eternal doctrine when he wrote the following: Our birth is but a sleep and a forgetting."

Eadie claims that this "forgetting" doctrine was something she gradually recalled throughout the course of her NDE. In describing our birth-induced memory loss, she calls it a "veil" of forgetfulness:

> Things were coming back to me from long before my life on earth, things that had been purposely blocked from me by a *"veil" of forgetfulness* at my birth.[22]

Did Eadie actually relearn this particular "truth" during her experience? At the time of her NDE she was already a member of the LDS church. As such, she would have been familiar with Mormon explanations of man's inability to remember the premortal world. They are strikingly similar to her words:

> [W]hen we are born into mortality a *veil* is drawn over our minds, so that we have *forgotten* our premortal life . . . (emphasis added).[23]
>
> [A]ll spirits who come here must come in complete *forgetfulness* of their pre-mortal existence. The purpose of a *veil* being drawn over their past experiences was to start all of God's children out . . . on as equal a basis as possible . . . (emphasis added).[24]

Before seeing what the Bible says about our origins, we must first take a look at another Mormon doctrine closely linked to the concept of a pre-earth life. It is the Mormon belief that God the Father is our *literal* Father, and as such, has a heavenly wife who is our *literal* Mother. This teaching, too, is contained in *Embraced By The Light*.

Our Heavenly Parents

The term "spiritual children" is not used figuratively by Mormons when they speak about our preexistence. In LDS theology, all of us are "literally sons and daughters of God."[25] "The designation *Father*," says Bruce McConkie, "is to be taken literally; it signifies that the Supreme Being is the literal Parent or Father of the spirits of all men. . . . All men, Christ included, were born as his children in pre-existence."[26] Joseph Fielding Smith said that God "is literally, and not in a figurative sense, our very Eternal Father."[27]

Eternal spirit matter (or "intelligence") was organized into these spirit children (or "intelligences") through sexual intercourse between God the Father and his celestial wife: "Our *spirit bodies* had their beginning in pre-existence when we were born as the spirit children of God our Father. Through that birth process spirit element was organized into intelligent entities."[28] Brigham Young stated the doctrine very clearly:

> He [God] created man, as we create our children; for there is no other process of creation in heaven, on the earth, in the earth, or under the earth, or in all the eternities, that is, that were, or that ever will be.[29]

Some Mormons have suggested that "Heavenly Father" may actually have *several* celestial wives[30] given the number of people who have been born. Officially, however, the Mormon god is a one-woman god:

> Implicit in the Christian verity that all men are the spirit children of an *Eternal Father* is the usually unspoken truth that they are also the offspring of an *Eternal Mother*. . . . This doctrine that there is a *Mother in Heaven* was affirmed in plainness by the First Presidency of the Church (Joseph F. Smith, John R. Winder, and Anthon H. Lund) when . . . they said that "man, as a spirit, was begotten and born of *heavenly parents*, and reared to maturity in the eternal mansions of the Father," that man is the "offspring of

celestial parentage," and that "all men and women are in the similitude of the *universal Father and Mother*, and are literally the sons and daughters of Deity."[31]

True to her LDS background, Eadie feels that God is "our mutual Father."[32] In one segment of her near-death narrative, she recounts how she "watched as our spirit brothers and sisters entered physical bodies for their turns upon earth."[33] While appearing on "The Oprah Winfrey Show," Eadie could not have made her views any plainer than when she said: "We are *literally* the children of God."[34]

Eadie says she also learned that we are not the *only* offspring of deity in the universe. There exist innumerable worlds in the great cosmos which have been populated by God through the aid of his Eternal Wife. "We are *all* God's children," says Eadie in describing her heavenly encounter with these distant relatives, "and he has filled the immensity of space for us."[35] She continues:

> I traveled tremendous distances, knowing that the stars I saw were not visible from earth. I saw galaxies and traveled to them with ease and almost instantaneous speed, visiting their worlds and meeting more children of our God, all of them our spiritual brothers and sisters.[36]

Eadie claims that the above knowledge was gained through her NDE.[37] But notice once more the similarity between her words and Mormon literature:

> We are blessed with the knowledge that ours is not the only inhabited *earth*. . . . The Father is the Creator of *worlds without number*. . . . They are inhabited by the spirit children of the Father. . . .[38]
> *We have brothers and sisters on other earths. They look like us because they, too, are the children of God* . . . they are also his offspring. His great work is to create earths and people them with his children who are called upon to pass through the mortal probation like unto this we are now in . . . .[39]

Eadie further promotes the LDS belief that Jesus received a spiritual body in heaven just like God's other spirit children received one. Jesus, she contends, is like everyone else, initially part of the whirling mass of thoughtless intelligence. Jesus only differs from us in that He was the very first spirit baby that Heavenly Father and Heavenly Mother formed from the spirit element.

Jesus is *literally* our big brother, according to Mormonism—"the most intelligent, the most faithful, and the most Godlike of all the sons and daughters of our Heavenly Father in the spirit world."[40] During an interview on WMUZ, Eadie shared how her NDE taught her this same thing. She learned that we are "literally His [God's] spiritual children . . . and that Jesus Christ *is our brother*."[41]

Mormons additionally view Jesus as their spiritual head. Consequently, they often say He possesses the qualities of not only an older brother, but also a father:

Mormonism	Embraced By The Light
CHRIST OUR ELDER BROTHER. . . . He is our *Elder Brother.* . . . Because of his divine authority and sacrifice on the cross, we become spiritually begotten sons and daughters, and *he is our Father* (emphasis added).[42]	. . . I developed a relationship and knowledge of the Savior that I will always cherish. . . . I felt that his relationship to me was both like a *father* and an *older brother* (pp. 72–73, emphasis added).

Eadie never mentions in her book exactly how Jesus got His *physical* body when He came to earth, but Mormon theology maintains that He was conceived through sexual intercourse between God the Father and Mary. In other words, when Mormons talk about the virgin birth, what they are actually saying is that Mary was a virgin when God the Father came to visit her, but she was not a virgin when He left.[43] This doctrine, rarely mentioned to non-Mormons, stems from the LDS idea that God the Father is a man (see Chapter 3):

> The birth of the Saviour was as natural as are the births of our children. . . . He partook of flesh and blood—was begotten of his Father, as we were of our fathers.[44]

> . . . I was naturally begotten; so was my father, and also my Saviour Jesus Christ. . . . he is the first begotten of his father in the flesh, and there was nothing unnatural about it.[45]

> . . . Christ was begotten by an Immortal Father in the same way that mortal men are begotten by mortal fathers.[46]

Next Stop, Planet Earth

Much of what Eadie believes must be carefully pieced together because *Embraced By The Light* is not written as a theology textbook. This, by the way, is why some doctrinal themes in her book are difficult to detect. Such is the case with her explanation of exactly how all of us came to earth and received our particular stations in life.

Eadie believes that we actually *chose* who we would be and what we would do. This position, however, varies somewhat from the standard Mormon explanation as the following comparison shows:

Mormonism	Embraced By The Light
. . . God stood in the midst of His spirit-children *and appointed* "the noble and great ones" to future positions . . . (emphasis added).[47]	[I]n the pre-mortal world *we knew about and even chose* our missions in life (p. 48, emphasis added).

(continued on next page)

Mormonism	Embraced By The Light
We have no scriptural justification, however, for the belief that we had the privilege of choosing our parents and our life companions in the spirit world.[48]	[W]e had bonded together in the spirit world with certain spirit brothers and sisters. . . . we covenanted with these spirits to come to earth as family or friends . . . chose to come to earth with certain others because of the work we would do (p. 92).

Although Eadie may somewhat disagree with what the LDS church officially says about the extent to which our free wills affect our earthly experiences, she does acknowledge the Mormon belief that spirits during the preearth life were valiant: "I knew that each of us who made the decision to come here was a *valiant* spirit," writes Eadie. "Even the least developed among us here was strong and *valiant* there" (p. 49—emphasis added).

This is one of Eadie's more disturbing references to her LDS faith because such terminology belies the Mormon explanation for why some people are black and why some people are white. Mormons believe that although everyone privileged to come to earth was indeed "valiant" in heaven, some spirits were *more* "valiant" and some were *less* "valiant." Those more "valiant" received the reward of a white body. Those less "valiant" received the curse of a black body.

The Ultimate Curse

Many claim that Mormonism and racism have been synonymous terms ever since Joseph Smith declared: "Had I anything to do with the negro, I would confine them by strict law to their own species . . . ."[49] Thelma "Granny" Geer, a fourth generation Mormon who eventually left the LDS church, explains in her book *Mormonism, Mama & Me* what it is like growing up Mormon:

As a white Mormon, I proudly accepted the teaching that my fair skin and Mormon parentage signified that I had been one of God's most intelligent and obedient born-in-heaven spirit children. . . . As a reward for my superior attributes and attitudes, I had been singled out, trained, and qualified to be born a white Latter-day Saint, deserving of emulation, adulation, and eventual deification. All dark-skinned people, even darker-complexioned Caucasians . . . had been inferior spirits in heaven .[50]

Mormons trace their Negroes-are-inferior doctrine to the premortal life. Joseph Fielding Smith explains:

There is a reason why one man is born black and with other disadvantages, while *another is born white* with great advantages. The reason is that we once had an estate before we came here, and were obedient, more or less, to the laws that were given us there. *Those who were faithful in all things there received greater blessings here, and those who were not faithful received less.*[51]

Latter-day Saints assert that our destiny here on earth was largely affected by our behavior during a great "rebellion in heaven" as well as during the heavenly war it sparked between Lucifer and Christ:

When the plan of redemption was presented and Jesus was chosen to be the Redeemer of the world, some rebelled. . . . In this great rebellion in heaven, Lucifer, or Satan . . . and one-third of the hosts thereof were cast out. . . . There were no neutrals in the war in heaven. *All took sides either with Christ or with Satan* . . . . The Negro, evidently, is receiving the reward he merits.[52]

Although every spirit who sided with Christ was valiant, some were less valiant than others. These spirits were supposedly condemned to live as Negroes:

Those who were less *valiant* in pre-existence . . .
are known to us as the *negroes.* Such spirits are sent
to earth through the lineage of Cain . . . are denied
the priesthood. . . . are not equal with other races
where the receipt of certain spiritual blessings are
concerned . . . this inequality is not of man's origin. It
is the Lord's doing . . . (emphasis added).[53]

LDS apostle Bruce McConkie penned the above words in
1966 when those of African descent were still not allowed to
hold the Mormon Priesthood (a very important LDS position
of blessings). On June 9, 1978, after mounting social pres-
sures, access to this Priesthood was finally opened up to all
Mormon males.

Such a politically correct move, however, could not erase
the prejudice that had been promoted by the Mormon
Church for nearly 140 years.

You see some classes of the human family that are
black, uncouth, uncomely, disagreeable, and low in
their habits, wild, and seemingly deprived of nearly
all the blessings of the intelligence that is generally
bestowed upon mankind. . . . Cain slew his
brother. . . . and the Lord put a mark on him, which
is the flat nose and black skin.[54]

Not only was Cain called upon to suffer, but because of his wickedness he became the father of an
inferior race.[55]

Shall I tell you the law of God in regard to the
African race? If the white man who belongs to the
chosen seed mixes his blood with the seed of Cain,
the penalty, under the law of God, is death on the
spot. This will always be so.[56]

[I]t has been the doctrine of the Church, never
questioned by any of the Church leaders, that the
Negroes are not entitled to the full blessings of the
Gospel. . . . your ideas, as we understand them, appear to contemplate the intermarriage of the Negro
and White races, a concept which has heretofore
been most repugnant to most normal-minded people
. . . . there is a growing tendency . . . toward the

breaking down of race barriers in the matter of inter-marriage between whites and blacks, but it does not have the sanction of the Church and is contrary to Church doctrine.[57]

Scripture plainly tells us that "God is no respecter of persons: But in every nation he that feareth him, and worketh righteousness, is accepted with him" (Acts 10:34–35, KJV). God's Word also informs us that there are absolutely no racial distinctions. "There is neither Jew nor Greek, there is neither bond nor free, there is neither male nor female: for ye are all one in Christ Jesus" (Galatians 3:28, KJV).

These points alone are enough to separate Mormonism from Christianity.

Nothing But the Bible

Mormon leader Milton R. Hunter writes: "When light burst forth from heaven in revelations to the Prophet Joseph Smith . . . . The stupendous truth of the existence of a Heavenly Mother, as well as a Heavenly Father, became established facts in Mormon theology."[58]

Brigham Young, in line with Smith's revelations about our preexistence, explained that people are "made first spiritual, and afterwards temporal [fleshly]."[59]

But Paul the apostle felt differently. He noted in his first letter to the Corinthians: "[T]hat was *not* first which was spiritual, but that which is natural; and afterward that which is spiritual" (1 Corinthians. 15:46, KJV, emphasis added). Paul is simply saying here that the natural, or physical, comes first, *then* comes the spiritual. Mormons claim the exact opposite.

Zechariah 12:1, in agreement with Paul, indicates that God forms the spirit within the body of each man and each woman on earth, rather than in the womb of a celestial Mother in heaven.

One biblical passage often cited by Mormons in support of their premortal doctrine is Jeremiah 1:5: "Before I formed thee in the belly I knew the; before thou camest forth out of the womb I sanctified thee, and I ordained thee a prophet . . ." (KJV).

55

In context, Jeremiah is not referring to a preearth life with God. The passage is speaking of God's omniscience (Psalm 139:11–12, 147:5; 1 John 3:19–20); specifically, His foreknowledge. The Old Testament prophet is addressing the fact that even before our births God knows everything about our lives—including our identity. He knows us as if we already existed. As Romans 4:17 puts it, God "calleth those things which be not as though they were" (KJV).

Isaiah 44:24 also contradicts the LDS doctrine of preexistence. Mormons, as we have shown, hold that all of us helped our heavenly Father in creation. Eadie agrees, claiming that all people as spirit children in the pre-mortal world "took part in the creation of the earth."[60] But Isaiah 44:24 reads: "I am the LORD, that maketh all things; that stretcheth forth the heavens alone: that spreadeth abroad the earth by myself . . ." (KJV).

Regarding our standing as God's children, Scripture nowhere states that we were procreated in the heavenly realms as *literal* sons and daughters of deity. Instead, we are described by the Bible as children of God by adoption (Romans 8:15).

We also know that Jesus was not organized in heaven from spirit matter into a spirit baby through procreation. The Bible says that He is the same yesterday, today, and forever (Hebrews 13:8). It would be a clear contradiction of this verse to maintain that Jesus changed in nature from an impersonal spirit element into a personal entity.

Preexistence and its accompanying doctrines are not the only Mormon teachings expressed in *Embraced By The Light*. Its pages subtly hide Polytheism (belief that there is more than one God), Finite Godism (belief that God progressed to godhood) and human deification (belief that all of us can one day reach the status of a god). It is to these Mormon heresies that our attention must now turn.

ENDNOTES

[1] Richards, Le Grand. *A Marvelous Work and A Wonder*, pp. 4–5.

[2] Eadie, Betty. *Embraced By The Light*, pp. 30–31.

[3] Schraffs, Gilbert W. *The Truth About "The Godmakers,"* pp. 92f as quoted in *Speaking the Truth in Love to Mormons* by Mark J. Cares, p. 16; cf. private letter from an LDS father to his adult daughter as quoted in *Speaking the Truth in Love to Mormons* by Mark J. Cares, p. 33; Pratt, Orson. *Journal of Discourses*, 19:320, "Discourse by Elder Orson Pratt, Delivered in the New Tabernacle, Salt Lake City, Oct. 7, 1867."

[4] Cares, Mark J. *Speaking the Truth in Love to Mormons*, p. 23.

[5] Schraffs, Gilbert W. *The Truth About "The Godmakers"* pp. 92f as quoted in *Speaking the Truth in Love to Mormons* by Mark J. Cares, p. 16

[6] Young, Brigham. *Journal of Discourses*, 1:349, "A Discourse by President Brigham Young, delivered in the Tabernacle, Great Salt Lake City, July 10, 1853."

[7] McConkie, Bruce. *Mormon Doctrine*, p. 240.

[8] Hunter, Milton R. *The Gospel Through the Ages*, p. 127.

[9] McConkie, op. cit., p. 589.

[10] Eadie, op. cit., p. 31.

[11] Ibid., p. 32.

[12] Ibid., p. 47.

[13] McConkie, op. cit., p. 169.

[14] Ibid., p. 590.

[15] Eadie, op. cit., pp. 47–48.

[16] McConkie, op. cit., p. 387.

[17] Ibid., p. 751.

[18] Ibid., p. 501.

[19] Eadie, op. cit., p. 97.

[20] Wordsworth, William. "Ode: Intimations of Immortality From Recollections of Early Childhood" as found in *Great Poems of the English Language*, compiled by Wallace Alvin Briggs, Volume 1, p. 415; cf. *The Norton Anthology of Poetry*, p. 552.

[21] Eadie, op. cit.

[22] Ibid., p. 44.

[23] Hunter, op. cit., p. 128.

[24] Ibid., p. 14.

[25] Ibid., p. 96.

[26] McConkie, op. cit., p. 278.

[27] Smith, Joseph Fielding. *Doctrines of Salvation*, 1:1.

[28] McConkie, op. cit., p. 750.

[29] Young, op. cit., 11:122, "Remarks by President Brigham Young, delivered in the Bowery, Great Salt Lake, June 18, 1865."

[30] Wilcox, Linda. *Sunstone*, "Mother in Heaven," Sept./Oct. 1980, p. 14; cf. Pratt, Orson. *The Seer*, "The Pre-Existence of Man," March 1853, pp. 37–39.

[31] McConkie, op. cit., p. 516.

[32] Eadie, op. cit., p. 47.

[33] Ibid., p. 52.

[34] "The Oprah Winfrey Show," 1/3/94 (re-aired 8/3/94).

[35] Eadie, op. cit., p. 88.

[36] Ibid.

[37] Ibid., pp. 88–89.

[38] McConkie, op. cit., p. 212.

[39] Smith, op. cit., 1:62.

[40] Hunter, op. cit., p. 21.

[41] Eadie, Betty. WMUZ 3/3/94 taped interview with Al Kresta.

[42] Smith, op. cit., 1:15, 29.

[43] Geer, Thelma "Granny." *Mormonism, Momma & Me*, pp. 91–92.

[44] Young, op. cit., 8:115, "Remarks by President Brigham Young, made in the Bowery, Great Salt Lake City, July 8, 1860."

[45] Kimball, Heber C. *Journal of Discourses*, 8:211, "Remarks by President Heber C. Kimball, made in the Bowery, Great Salt Lake City, September 2, 1860."

[46] McConkie, op. cit., p. 547.

[47] Hunter, op. cit., p. 15.

[48] Smith, Joseph Fielding. *The Way to Perfection*, p. 44.

[49] Smith, Joseph. *Documentary History of the Church*, January 2, 1843 speech as quoted in *Teachings of the Prophet Joseph Smith*, edited by Joseph Fielding Smith, p. 276.

[50] Geer, op. cit., pp. 24–25.

[51] Smith, *Doctrines of Salvation*, 1:61.

[52] Ibid., 1:64–66.

[53] McConkie, op. cit., p. 527.

[54] Young, op. cit., 7:290, "Remarks by President Brigham Young, delivered in the Tabernacle, Great Salt Lake City, October 9, 1859."

[55] Smith, Joseph Fielding, op. cit., p. 101.

[56] Young, op. cit., 10:110, "Remarks by President Brigham Young, made in the Tabernacle, Great Salt Lake City, March 8, 1863."

[57] LDS First Presidency. 7/17/47 letter from LDS First Presidency to Dr. Lowery Nelson as quoted in *Mormonism and the Negro* by John J. Steward and William E. Barrett, Part 1, p. 47.

[58] Hunter, op. cit., p. 98.

[59] Young, op. cit., 1:50, "A sermon delivered by President Brigham Young, in the Tabernacle, Great Salt Lake City, April 9, 1852."

[60] Eadie, op. cit., p. 47.

CHAPTER 3

From Utah with Love

*Beloved, let us love one another; for love is of God; and
every one that loveth is born of God, and knoweth God.
He that loveth not knoweth not God; for God is love.*

— 1 John 4:7–8, KJV

I contacted Betty Eadie by telephone in January of 1994
and spoke with her for nearly an hour. "Why did you
write *Embraced By The Light?*" I asked.

She responded, "Well, I had this wonderful experience
that I believe was given to me from God and I felt like I had
to share it."

"What is the main message of your book?"

"Love," Eadie said. "Learn to love one another."

Her answer did not surprise me. She had written essentially the same thing in the final pages of *Embraced By The
Light*: "We are to love one another. . . . We are to be kind, to
be tolerant, to give generous service. . . . greater joy will
come to us through love than in any other way. . . . The
details of my experience are important only to the point that
they help us to love. . . . 'Above all else, love one another.' "[1]

Although Eadie's admonition seems filled with wisdom
from above, it lacks substance because she makes no mention of whose definition of love we are to use. In the 1969
blockbuster movie entitled *Love Story*, Ryan O'Neal and Ali
McGraw said love is "never having to say you're sorry." Ac-

cording to vocalist Bette Midler, love is a flower; "a rose" to be exact.

Besides leaving love undefined, Eadie has also neglected to fully explain the foundation upon which love is to be based. She gives no sufficient grounds for why anyone should begin loving, or continue loving, at all. Eadie did tell me during our conversation, however, that the Bible was extremely important.[2] It might be that she feels God is the one who defines love.

But this presents another series of questions left unanswered: Which god? The Hindu god? The Buddhist god? The Muslim god? Eadie has avoided addressing these very important issues, but a careful examination of *Embraced By The Light* reveals that it is primarily the Mormon god to whom she is looking for love.

God Is Just a Man

Ask any Latter-day Saint to describe his or her faith and you will probably receive a response that sounds something like: *"Mormonism is Christianity; Christianity is Mormonism; they are one and the same, and they are not to be distinguished from each other in the minutest detail."*[3]

Many Mormons may indeed *act* Christian by being kind, helping those in need, obeying the laws of the land and speaking out against evils such as pornography. But good behavior does not make them Christian. A person's Christianity is dependent upon whether or not he or she has a personal relationship with God through a life-changing faith that has been placed solely in the person and work of Jesus Christ.

Latter-day Saints often say that they do, in fact, have a personal relationship with God. What they unfortunately fail to see is that it is not the *Christian* God with whom they have a relationship. They have a "relationship" with the Mormon god who is nothing more than "an exalted, glorified, and perfected Man."[4]

An oft-quoted speech delivered by Joseph Smith at an LDS conference held in Nauvoo, Illinois on April 6, 1844, gives perhaps the clearest and most concise explanation possible of the Mormon doctrine of deity:

God Himself was once as we are now, and is an exalted Man. . . . if you were to see him today, you would see him like a man in form—like yourselves, in all the person, image, and very form as a man. . . . We have imagined and supposed that God was God from all eternity, I will refute that idea. . . . he was once a man like us; yea, that God himself the Father of us all, dwelt on an earth the same as Jesus Christ himself did . . . .[5]

Brigham Young, Smith's successor, preached:

If our Father and God should be disposed to walk through one of these aisles, we should not know him from one of the congregation. You would see a man, and that is all you would know about him; you would merely know him as a stranger from some neighboring city or country. This is the character of Him whom we worship and acknowledge as our Father and God . . . .[6]

In *The Gospel Through the Ages*, Mormon apostle Milton R. Hunter articulates what God had to do in order to become God:

[H]ow did He [God] become glorified and exalted and attain His present status of Godhood? . . . aeons ago God undoubtedly took advantage of every opportunity to learn the laws of truth and as He became acquainted with each new verity He righteously obeyed it. . . . He exerted His will vigorously. . . . As he gained more knowledge through persistent effort and continuous industry, as well as through absolute obedience, His understanding of the universal laws continued to become more complete. Thus He grew in experience and continued to grow until He attained the status of Godhood.[7]

Scripture explicitly says that God is not a man (Numbers 23:19; 1 Samuel 15:29; Hosea 11:9). The Bible also tells us that God has always been God (Isaiah. 41:4, 57:15; Romans 16:26). In the words of Psalms 90:2 and 93:2, God has been God "from eternity to eternity." He is unchanging (Malachi 3:6; Hebrews 6:17–18; James 1:17).

The Mormon idea that God has a body of flesh and bones because he is a man[8] is also contradicted by Scripture. John 4:24 says God is a spirit, and Jesus taught in Luke 24:39 that a spirit does not have flesh and bones.

Betty Eadie Versus the Trinity

Latter-day Saints will often describe the exalted man whom they worship as a "personage" entirely separate and distinct from Jesus Christ. Such a theological position comes not from Scripture, but from a vision of the Father and the Son which Joseph Smith claimed to have had in 1820.

Smith's grandnephew, Joseph Fielding Smith, states: "The vision of Joseph Smith made it clear that the Father and the Son are separate personages, having bodies as tangible as the body of man."[9]

Virtually all Mormons know that their Jesus-is-a-separate-being-from-the-Father doctrine comes directly from Smith's 1820 vision. This because membership in the church is obtained only after baptism,[10] which is itself received only after learning all of the church's central teachings, and no teaching is more central to Mormonism than Joseph Smith's "First Vision." In fact, it is considered by Mormons to be "one of the most important and momentous events in this world's history."[11]

According to an interview with her in *Salt Lake Tribune*, Eadie had already converted from Protestantism to Mormonism before "dying."[12] A *Deseret News* article of January 17, 1993 confirms that at the time of her NDE she was an "inactive Mormon" and that afterwards she "became active in the LDS faith, finding joy in speaking to many groups about her experience."[13] Given this fact, one can only wonder how Eadie could say that it was during her NDE that she learned about the Father and Son. "I understood, *to my surprise*," writes Eadie, "that Jesus was a separate being from God . . ." (emphasis added).[14]

Eadie goes on to comment on how this "new-found truth" about the Father and Jesus Christ contradicted her Protestant upbringing, which taught her that "God the Father and Jesus Christ were one being."[15] Eadie's obvious allusion to the Trinity doctrine again reflects her LDS beliefs. (Note: Orthodox Christianity, or Protestantism, does *not* teach that Jesus Christ and the Father are "one being" in the same sense Eadie implies [i.e., that Jesus is the Father].)

Mormons have historically belittled the Christian position that there is only *one* God who exists as three distinct persons. Joseph Smith, for example, declared:

> Many men say there is one God; the Father, the Son and the Holy Ghost are only one God. I say that is a strange God anyhow—three in one, and one in three! . . . All are to be crammed into one God. . . . It would make the biggest God in all the world. He would be a wonderfully big God—he would be a giant or a monster.[16]

Eadie's Mormon view of the Trinity also surfaced when, during a 3/3/94 interview with WMUZ talk-show host Al Kresta, she attempted to explain the nature of the godhead. Kresta picked up on Eadie's Mormon-sounding definition of the Trinity and asked about it. Eadie was again evasive. She denied having any knowledge of the Mormon doctrine of deity at the time of her NDE:[17]

> *EADIE* The best way that I could describe that [Trinity] would be going back to the parents; where you have the father, the mother and the child. They are all one perhaps in purpose, perhaps in family membership they are all one. But separately they are individual.
> *KRESTA* This is similar then to fairly traditional Mormonism. Is that right?
> *EADIE* [pause] Well, I, I have been hearing that. And also as well as uhm, ah, let's see what's the other? There's yoga. Uhm, there's Buddhism or Muslim, or whatever. I mean, just about [does not finish]. I am so surprised at the common threads that run through

all belief systems. Ah, I am even more surprised that people have not, ah, become aware of that. That basically they believe that it only exists in their particular religion. Where, as I understand, this goes way, way back beyond Mormonism. Beyond ah, ah, it goes way back into China somewhere and I can't recall off the top of my head where this originated.

KRESTA But you weren't conscious of this deriving from Mormonism?

EADIE No, I was not.

Eadie gave me virtually the same answer when, during our interview, I made an observation similar to Kresta's:[18]

ABANES There are many things in your book that do sound very reminiscent of the faith practiced by the Church of Jesus Christ of Latter-day Saints.

EADIE That's what I've been told. As well as the Muslims, and the Buddhists. . . . I've gotten some responses from Christian Scientists as well.

The orthodox definition of the Trinity asserts that there is only one true God who, within His eternal nature, exists as three distinct persons (or three centers of consciousness); namely, the Father, the Son, and the Holy Spirit. Although these coequal and coeternal Persons are distinct in function, position and relationship, they all share the same nature, or essence. They *are* the one God.

Some object to this doctrine because the term "trinity" is not found in Scripture. But this objection has no real merit. The word "trinity" is simply a word that makes it easier for someone to refer to the Bible's rather complex teachings on God's nature. An analogy may help.

Water is two parts hydrogen and one part oxygen, yet one would never say: "May I please have a glass of two parts hydrogen and one part oxygen?" Instead, the simple term "water" is used for the sake of convenience. This is how the word "trinity" is used.

It is fairly easy to determine logically whether or not the Trinity doctrine is found in God's Word. If Scripture indicates that there exists three distinct persons (the Father, the

Son and the Holy Spirit) and each person is called God, but the Bible also states that there is only one *true* God, then logically, since neither the Father nor the Son nor the Holy Spirit is a false god, all of them must *somehow* be the one true God.

To demonstrate the Trinity, then, we need to find three things in Scripture: 1) three distinct Persons mentioned; 2) each person being called God; and 3) indications that there is only one God. The following represents only a few of the several hundred verses which demonstrate the Trinity:

1. Three distinct persons
   A. The Father (1 John 3:1)
   B. The Son (1 John 1:3)
   C. The Holy Spirit (the following verses are applicable only to a personal being)
      1. Personal pronouns used of (John 14:6, 26; 15:26; 16:13-14)
      2. Can be lied to (Acts 5:32)
      3. Feels love (Romans 15:30) and can be grieved (Ephesians 4:30)
2. Each person called God
   A. The Father (1 Thessalonians 1:1)
   B. The Son (John 1:1; 20:28; Hebrews 1:8, 9)
   C. The Holy Spirit (Acts 5: 3-4)
3. There is only one God (Deuteronomy. 4:35, 39; Psalm 86:10; Isaiah 45:5, 22)

Many find the Trinity difficult to understand because they mistakenly view the "persons" within God's nature the same way they view *human* persons. The terms, however, are not used identically. In reference to God, the word "persons" is simply the best word available to indicate God's three distinct centers of consciousness, which can somehow interact (John 10:15; 17:8), love one another (John 3:35; 5:20), cooperate with each other (John 8:15–18), and function independently (John 20:21) while at the same time sharing the same nature, or essence (John 10:30–33).

The Trinity is not an easy doctrine to fully comprehend, but this does not mean that it cannot be understood to a reasonable degree. Understanding something, while at the same time not being able to fully comprehend exactly how that something can be, are compatible states of mind.

For example, I may *understand* that this earth is revolving at a speed of several thousands of miles per hour, but I certainly do not *comprehend* how that can be. I may also *understand* that the chair on which I am sitting is comprised of millions of molecules moving so fast that they are forming only what looks like a solid object, but I certainly do not *comprehend* how that can be.

If we are willing to accept these things without full comprehension of them, it is only fair that we give the same level of consideration to the doctrine of the Trinity despite our inability to *fully* comprehend it. Besides, God has explicitly told us that certain aspects of His nature are unsearchable (Psalm 145:3; Isaiah 40:28; Romans 11:33).

The question to ask is not: *How* does the Trinity exist? But simply: *Does* the Trinity exist? According to Scripture, the answer to the latter question is yes. For those whose minds cannot let go of the former question, there is an analogy for the Trinity which may be helpful: "time."

First, "time" consists of three distinct things: past, present, and future. These three aspects of "time" correspond well to the Trinity's Father, Son and Holy Spirit. In both cases the three aspects are distinct from one another.

Second, all three aspects of "time," although distinct, share the same nature of that which they comprise. In other words, the past, present and future can all be referred to individually as "time" just like the Father, Son and Holy Spirit can each be referred to as God.

Third, if any of the three elements of "time" were to be removed, "time" would no longer exist. In this dimension of reality, there is no such thing as "time" without a past, a present, or a future. Similarly, God would not be God without a Father, a Son or a Holy Spirit. All three persons *are* God, just as all three aspects of "time" *are* "time."

Belief in the Trinity is the sole theological view able to reconcile the Scriptures which call three persons God, with the Scriptures which say there is only one God. Otherwise the only logical option would be to dismiss Scripture as a document full of contradictions.

Polytheism á la Eadie

While Mormons accept the biblical verses affirming the plurality of God, they deny any passages which demonstrate His unity. In other words, they reject the Scriptures which show that there is only one God, choosing instead to believe that the Father, Son and Holy Ghost are three gods. *Mormon Doctrine* reads: "As pertaining to this universe, there are three Gods: the Father, Son, and Holy Ghost."[19]

This belief, like nearly every other Mormon doctrine, originated with Joseph Smith. "I have always declared God to be a distinct personage," said Smith on June 16, 1844. "Jesus Christ a separate and distinct personage from God the Father, and that the Holy Ghost was a distinct personage and a spirit: and these three constitute three distinct personages and three Gods."[20]

Although Eadie never mentions the Holy Spirit in *Embraced By The Light*, she does talk about Jesus in LDS fashion when she says on page 44: "I understood that he was the Son of God, though he himself was also a God . . . ."[21]

Notice the phraseology. Eadie says "a" god, indicating that Jesus is "a" god who is separate from God the Father. Eadie personally explained to me that Jesus is indeed "a" god and that above him is another god whom she described as "His Father, our Father."[22]

Christians, because they believe in only one God, are monotheists. (Monotheism is defined as belief in one God.) Mormons, because they believe in more than one God, are polytheists. (Polytheism is defined as belief in more than one god.)

Latter-day Saints, including Eadie, believe in at least three gods: the Father, Son and Holy Ghost. But there are far more gods than this, according to Mormon theology. LDS Apostle Orson Pratt theorized, "If we should take a million of worlds like this and number their particles, we should find that there are more Gods than there are particles of matter in those worlds."[23]

Brigham Young, much less willing to make estimates about the number of gods in existence, would only say, "How many gods there are I do not know. But there never was a time when there were not gods . . . ."[24]

Several Scriptures have already been given which show that there is only one God. Another verse, however, is especially damaging to Mormon theology if taken in light of something written by Mormon leader Joseph Fielding Smith: "I believe that *God knows all things* and that *his understanding is perfect, not 'relative'. . . . He comprehendeth all things*, and all things are before him . . . ."[25]

This statement cancels out the LDS doctrine of many gods when coupled with what the Lord said in Isaiah 44:8: ". . . ye are even my witnesses. Is there a God beside me? . . . I know not any." God, who knows all things, reveals in His Word that He knows of no other Gods.

That there is only one God cannot be made any clearer (1 Timothy 2:5). "Even the demons believe that—and shudder" (James 2:19).

ENDNOTES

[1] Eadie, Betty. *Embraced By The Light*, p. 147.

[2] Eadie, Betty. Author's 1/25/94 interview with Eadie.

[3] McConkie, Bruce. *Mormon Doctrine*, p. 513.

[4] Ibid., p. 751.

[5] Smith, Joseph. *Journal of Discourses*, 6:3–4, "A Discourse, by President Joseph Smith, delivered at the Conference held near the Temple, in Nauvoo, April 6, 1844."

[6] Young, Brigham. *Journal of Discourses*, 11:40, "Remarks by President Brigham Young, delivered in the Tabernacle, Great Salt Lake City, Jan. 8, 1865."

[7] Hunter, Milton, R. *The Gospel Through the Ages*, pp. 114-115.

[8] Smith, Joseph. *Doctrine & Covenants* 130:22.

[9] Smith, Joseph Fielding. *Doctrines of Salvation*, 1:2.

[10] LDS Church. *Gospel Principles*, p. 127.

[11] Richards, Le Grand. *A Marvelous Work and A Wonder*, p. 6.

[12] Phillips, Valerie. [Ogden]*Standard-Examiner*, "Author Shares Love of Life After Death in an Embrace," 3/6/93, n.p.

[13] Boren, Karen. *Deseret News*, "Is Death Merely the Precipice of True Birth?" 1/17/93, n.p.

[14] Eadie, *Embraced*, p. 47.

[15] Ibid.

[16] Smith, Joseph. *Documentary History of the Church*, "Sermon by the Prophet—The Christian Godhead—Plurality of Gods," June 16, 1844 as quoted in *Teachings of the Prophet Joseph Smith*, edited by Joseph Fielding Smith, p. 372.

[17] Eadie, Betty. WMUZ 3/3/94 taped interview with Al Kresta.

[18] Eadie, author's 1/25/94 interview, op. cit

[19] McConkie, op. cit., p. 270.

[20] Smith, *Documentary History of the Church*, op. cit., p. 370.

[21] Eadie, *Embraced*, p. 44.

[22] Eadie, author's 1/25/94 interview, op. cit

[23] Pratt, Orson. *Journal of Discourses*, 2:345, "A Discourse by Elder Orson Pratt, Delivered in the open air, on the Temple Block, Great Salt Lake City, February 18, 1855."

[24] Young, op. cit., 7:333, "Remarks by President Brigham Young, delivered in the Tabernacle, Great Salt Lake City, October 8, 1859."

[25] Smith, Joseph Fielding, op. cit., 1:8–9.

CHAPTER 4

Eternity to Eternity

[S]ince mortal beings are the spirit children of Heavenly Parents . . . the ultimate possibility is for some of them to become exalted to Godhood.

— Milton R. Hunter, Mormon Apostle[1]

Before going any further, it might be best to summarize the Mormon doctrines we have thus far discussed:

• God, before he was God, existed as an ordinary man.
• After aeons of time, He became an *exalted* man. In other words, a god.
• En route to deification, God acquired a wife (or wives).
• Before being born on earth, all of us were born in heaven as spirit babies. Our Father and Mother god procreated billions of spirit children through celestial sex. Although heavenly intercourse was the means through which we were created, the raw material out of which we were formed was preexisting "spirit matter" called "intelligence."
• We have a *literal* Father and Mother in heaven.
• During the preearth life all of us had relationships with each other as well as with our Heavenly Parents.

Our actions in that preearth life determined the race into which we were born.

• There is a countless number of gods throughout the universe.

Mormons refer to the path traveled by God toward deification as "eternal progression." This process, which everyone goes through, is why there are so many gods in existence. If all goes well, each person will obtain exaltation (godhood) just like God the Father. It is a "gradually unfolding course of advancement and experience—a course that began in a past eternity [preexistence] and will continue in ages future ...."[2] Joseph Smith declared:

> [Y]ou have got to learn how to be Gods yourselves ... the same as all Gods have done before you— namely, by going from one small degree to another, and from one small capacity to a great one ....[3]

Becoming a god is what being a Mormon is all about. According to McConkie, "That exaltation which the saints of all ages have so devoutly sought is *godhood* itself."[4] The reward for reaching such a goal is definitely appealing:

> Godhood is to have the character, possess the attributes, and enjoy the perfections which the Father has. It is to do what he does, have the powers resident in him, and live as he lives ....[5]
>
> Those who obtain exaltation will gain all power and thus themselves be omnipotent.[6]

As pleasing as this reward may be, the main benefit of deification is the ability to create spirit babies through eternal sex just like "Heavenly Father" has done:

> [E]xaltation consists in the continuation of the family unit in eternity. . . . Those who obtain it. . . . have spirit children in the resurrection, in relation to which offspring they stand in the same position that God our Father stands to us.[7]

Of course, achieving godhood through "eternal progression" does not happen overnight. It takes "eternities" to become a god:

> [M]an began his progression and advancement in pre-existence. . . . he gains a mortal body, receives experience in earthly things, and prepares for a future eternity. . . . past ages when all men dwelt in the presence of their Eternal Father were one eternity, and those future ages when these spirit children will have gone on to exaltation, having spirit children of their own, will be another eternity.[8]

Eadie also believes in eternal progression, and makes numerous references to it in *Embraced By The Light* :

Mormonism	*Embraced By The Light*
[C]oming to earth to prove oneself is a prerequisite to *eternal progression* . . . (emphasis added).[9]	[A]n individual raises his level of understanding about God and his own *eternal progress*. . . (p. 45, emphasis added).
Man . . . was begotten and born of Heavenly Parents . . . prior to coming *upon the earth* in a temporal body to undergo an *experience*. . . (emphasis added).[10]	[O]ur spirit brothers and sisters entered physical bodies for their turns *upon earth*, each *experiencing* the pains and joys that would help them *progress* (p. 52, emphasis added).
[God and Jesus] have been forever reaching downward to mortals to assist them in their eternal struggle for *progres-*	They [Eadie's family] have begun their own families and embarked on their own paths of

(continued on next page)

Mormonism	Embraced By The Light
sion toward Godhood (emphasis added).[11]	*progression* (p. 146, emphasis added).
The process of gaining exaltation consists in growing in *knowledge* until a state of godhood is reached (emphasis added).[12]	The more *knowledge* we acquire here, the further and faster we will *progress* . . . (p. 84, emphasis added).
[T]he Father is the Creator of *worlds without number*. . . . they are inhabited by the spirit children of the Father. . . . man began his *progression* and advancement in pre-existence, his ultimate goal being to attain a state of glory, honor, and exaltation *like the Father* . . . (emphasis added).[13]	I had seen people *progressing* in the *worlds* I had visited, working toward becoming more *like our Father* . . . (p. 89, emphasis added).

According to Eadie, we mortals actually "need the spirits on the other side for our progression." These spirits, she says, "are *very* happy to assist us in any way they can."[14]

Understanding eternal progression is crucial to Mormons because "for the overwhelming majority of mankind, *eternal progression* has very definite limitations. In the full sense, *eternal progression* is enjoyed only by those who receive exaltation....Those who gain exaltation, having thus enjoyed the fulness of *eternal progression*, become like God" (emphasis added).[15]

Inseparable from man's eternal progression (reaching toward godhood) is the exclusively Mormon concept of "agency" (something akin to free will) which is given to each person in the premortal life. Note how closely Eadie's book reflects her Mormon faith:

Mormonism	Embraced By The Light
Free *agency* was given unto man that he might *act for himself* . . . (emphasis added).[16]	We are given *agency to act for ourselves* here (p. 49, emphasis added).
[T]he *free agency* of man, as expressed in *individual will*, has continued in mortality as a basic principle in the eternal law of progression (emphasis added). [17]	He [God] will give us all the help he can without interfering in our *personal agency* and *free will* (p. 101, emphasis added).
. . . God will increase His glory by assisting His children to become *as He is*.[18] [S]pirit children were organized, possessing, divine, eternal, and *godlike attributes* . . . (emphasis added).[19]	I understood . . . God wants us to become *as he is*, and that he has invested us with *god-like qualities* . . . (p. 61, emphasis added).
[I]n accordance with the inviolable *law of organic nature*—that like beget like. . . . "each *after his kind*," the child may achieve the former status of the parent . . . man is a God in embryo (emphasis added).[20]	Everything produces *after its own kind*. This too is a *spiritual law* (p. 66, emphasis added).

At a large 1975 gathering of Latter-day Saints, the 12th president of the Mormon church—Spencer W. Kimball—gleefully proclaimed: "Brethren, 225,000 of you are here tonight. I suppose 225,000 of you may become gods. There seems to be plenty of space out there in the universe."[21]

God Himself, however, declares in Isaiah 43:10, ". . . before me there was no God formed, neither shall there be after me" (KJV).

Another problem Mormons face concerning their hope to become like god is related to their belief that they will actually share in God's glory upon reaching deification. LDS apostle James Talmage writes: "We believe in a God who is Himself progressive, . . . a Being who has attained His exalted state by a path which now His children are permitted to follow, whose glory it is their heritage to share."[22]

Contradicting this Mormon thought is Isaiah 42:8 and Isaiah 48:10–11, which indicate that God will share His glory with no one. Even if for the sake of discussion we were to allow for such claims of eventual godhood, Mormons would still fall under the fearful condemnation reserved for "gods" who did not single-handedly create the heavens and the earth. Latter-day Saints will readily admit that they did not make the heavens and the earth by themselves. This being the case, Jeremiah 10:11 should be of great interest to them. It promises: "Thus shall ye say unto them, 'the gods that have not made the heavens and the earth, even they shall perish from the earth, and from under these heavens' " (KJV).

In the Beginning

The doctrine of eternal progression ultimately denies the Christian concept of the Fall in the Garden of Eden. According to eternal progression, Adam and Eve did not really "fall," but instead sort of stumbled upwards. Their disobedience was all part of God's wonderful plan to get His spirit children moving toward godhood. The Fall was actually a blessed event rather than a tragic one:

> According to the foreordained plan, Adam was to fall . . . Adam was to introduce immortality . . . so that the opportunity for eternal progression and perfection might be offered to all the spirit children of the Father.[23]

When Adam was driven out of the Garden of Eden,
the Lord passed a sentence upon him. Some people
have looked upon that sentence as being a dreadful
thing. It was not; it was a blessing.[24]

Mormons say that what transpired in the Garden was not
even sinful. The Fall was good fortune because it changed
Adam and Eve from immortal beings into mortal beings,
thereby enabling us, as their descendants, to also obtain
mortality, which is an essential experience for godhood.
Joseph Fielding Smith's explanation of the Fall is very
similar to Eadie's explanation:

Joseph Fielding Smith	Betty Eadie
I never speak of the part Eve took in this fall as a sin, nor do I accuse Adam. . . . When he ate, he became subject to death, and therefore he became mortal. . . . neither Adam nor Eve looked upon it as a sin . . . . The fall . . . brought to pass all of the vicissitudes [changes] of mortality. . . . It brought death; but we must not lose sight of the fact that it brought blessings. . . .[25]	Eve did not "fall" to temptation as much as she made a conscious decision to bring about conditions necessary for her progression, and her initiative was used to finally get Adam to partake of the fruit. In their partaking of the fruit, then, they brought mankind to mortality, which gave us conditions necessary for having children—but also to die.[26]

Smith makes no mention of children, but one need only
turn to the LDS doctrinal manual *Gospel Principles* to find a
comment almost identical to Eadie's:

When Adam and Eve were placed in the Garden of
Eden they were not yet mortal. They were not able to
have children. . . . Their physical condition changed
as a result of their eating the forbidden fruit. As God

had promised, they became mortal. They were able to have children. They and their children could experience sickness, pain, and physical death.[27]

The Book of Mormon also explains that "if Adam had not transgressed he would not have fallen. . . . And they would have had no children . . . ."[28]

Intimately tied to this view is the assertion that man is innately good. High-ranking Mormon Boyd Packer writes: "It is critically important that you understand that you already know right from wrong, that you're innately, inherently, and intuitively good."[29]

Eadie shares Boyd's sentiment: "I was gratified to see that the earth is only a temporary place for our schooling and that sin is not our true nature."[30]

The Bible, however, teaches that Adam and Eve's disobedience was a sinful act through which sin and death spread to all men (Romans 5:12; 6:23). Eve did not make a good choice. She was deceived, and Adam deliberately disobeyed the Lord (Genesis 3:13; 1 Timothy 2:14).

Furthermore, man is not innately good. He is inherently evil (Psalm 58:2–3; Ecclesiastes 9:3; Jeremiah 17:9). His heart continually shuns God and seeks to do only wrong (Genesis 6:5; Psalm 14:3; Isaiah 53:1–3; John 3:19; Romans 3:11–12). No one is righteous (Ecclesiastes 7:20; Isaiah 64:6; Romans 3:23). In fact, Paul the apostle called men slaves to sin (Romans 6:6, 17, 20).

"O wretched man that I am," wrote Paul in his letter to the Romans. "Who shall deliver me from the body of this death? I thank God—through Jesus Christ our Lord" (Romans 7:24–25, KJV). This is the good news, or the gospel, which Paul preached: "Christ died for our sins according to the scriptures; And that he was buried, and that he rose again the third day according to the scriptures" (1 Corinthians 15:3–4, KJV).

LDS Apostle George Q. Cannon explained that the gospel of Mormonism (and Betty Eadie) is altogether different: "Who is there that believes more in true evolution than the Latter-day Saints—The evolution of man until he shall become a God. . . . That is the gospel of Jesus Christ believed by the Latter-day Saints."[31]

Mormonism's divinity of man doctrine is the same lie used to deceive Adam and Eve in the Garden of Eden (Genesis 3:5). Because it is the same lie, it will produce the same results—physical and spiritual death. Psalm 82 reveals that all men, regardless of whether or not they call themselves gods, will die as men.

Paul, in his letter to the Galatians wrote, "If anybody is preaching to you a gospel other than what you accepted, let him be eternally condemned" (Galatians 1:9).

If such a severe condemnation is upon those who preach one false gospel, we can only speculate as to the end that awaits those individuals who preach several false gospels. Betty Eadie not only promotes the Mormon gospel, but also spreads the false teachings of the New Age movement.

ENDNOTES

[1] Hunter, Milton R. *The Gospel Through the Ages*, p. 104.

[2] McConkie, Bruce. *Mormon Doctrine*, p. 238.

[3] Smith, Joseph. *Journal of Discourses*, 6:4, "A Discourse, by President Joseph Smith, delivered at the Conference held near the Temple, in Nauvoo, April 6, 1844."

[4] McConkie, op. cit., p. 321.

[5] Ibid.

[6] Ibid., p. 544.

[7] Ibid., p. 257.

[8] Ibid., pp. 238, 240.

[9] LDS Church. *Student Manual*, "Old Testament: Genesis–2 Samuel," p. 31.

[10] Hunter, op. cit., p. 99.

[11] Ibid., pp. 52–53.

[12] McConkie, op. cit., p. 426.

[13] Ibid., pp. 212, 238.

[14] Eadie, Betty. *Embraced By The Light*, p. 48.

[15] McConkie, op. cit., p. 239.

[16] Smith, Joseph Fielding. *The Way to Perfection*, p. 28.

[17] Hunter, op. cit., p. 17.

[18] Ibid., p. 8.

[19] Ibid., p. 127.

[20] Talmage, James A. *A Study of the Articles of Faith*, p. 529.

[21] Kimball, Spencer W. *Ensign*, "The Privilege of Holding the Priesthood," 11/75, p. 80.

[22] Talmage, op. cit., p. 430.

[23] McConkie, op. cit., p. 268.

[24] Smith, Joseph Fielding. *Doctrines of Salvation*, 1:113.

[25] Ibid., 1:114–115.

[26] Eadie, op. cit., p. 109.

[27] LDS Church. *Gospel Principles*, pp. 30–31.

[28] Smith, Joseph. *The Book of Mormon*, 2 Nephi 2:22–25 as quoted in *Gospel Principles* by the LDS Church, p. 31.

[29] LDS Church. *Duties and Blessings of the Priesthood*, Part B, p. 186.

[30] Eadie, op. cit., pp. 49–50.

[31] Cannon, George Q. *Gospel Truths*, 1:9.

PART 2

"THE LIGHT"
OF
THE NEW AGE

No Christian is immune from exposure to New Age influences. This is because some New Agers consider themselves Christians, and thus move about in Christian as well as New Age circles. Furthermore, many Christians are unclear as to exactly what is unchristian about the New Age, and thus ignorantly absorb and then impart such influences to other Christians.

— Elliot Miller, New Age expert[1]

CHAPTER 5

"San Francisco, Here I Come"

While society today struggles to deal with murder, destruction, and moral decay, a book has emerged that offers a message of hope, light, and love. Embraced By The Light *teaches that there is purpose to this life, that we each have a specific reason for being here, and that "above all else, we must learn to love one another." Ms. Eadie has been traveling extensively this past year. . . . We invite you to come and meet Betty on Saturday at the Whole Life Expo.*

— *Program Guide*, 1994 Whole Life Expo[2]

The alarm's high-pitched beeps sounded at 3 a.m. "Already?" I thought, as I nudged my wife. "Bri, it's time to get up."

Bri's lack of response suggested that the weekend might not start off as early as planned.

"Hey, come on. We have to beat traffic."

The next thing I clearly recall is looking at my watch while driving away from our apartment complex at 4 a.m.

We were off to the San Francisco Spring Whole Life Expo, an annual event where participants in the New Age movement (commonly called New Agers) come together in a convention-like setting to promote their particular paths to physical healing, mental wholeness and spiritual enlightenment. Planners of the 1994 gathering had promised: "It is our intention to provide you with an event of truly uncommon value from which you can continue to benefit for years to come."[3]

By noon, Bri and I were experiencing the sights and sounds of Fisherman's Wharf in America's "City by the Bay." Not until the next day, however, would our *spiritual* senses be stirred by the New Age Fair. I could hardly wait to see if the Expo staff would make good on their pledge to provide an event of truly "uncommon" value. The following morning brought us to downtown San Francisco's Fashion Center, a megastructure housing the Expo's exhibitions. Its seemingly endless floor space, partitioned and squared off like mini tracts of land, served as a base of operations for New Agers peddling everything from acupuncture to Zen.

Many of those present were psychic healers and counselors. Their rented booths were everywhere. Equally plentiful in number were the herbalists and vegetarians who had strategically placed themselves next to the All Natural Food Pavilion. Channelers—individuals who allow themselves to be possessed by spirits in order to receive supernatural messages—were also present. For less adventuresome New Agers, there was a host of mediums utilizing more traditional means of divination (e.g., tarot cards, crystal balls and palm-reading).

Those needing a break from this "bustling marketplace" of vendors—as the Expo's "Imagine A World of Possibilities" *Program Guide* called it—could enjoy hourly lectures by well-known New Age personalities.

Page 35 of the *Program Guide* listed Terry Cole-Whittaker. Her lecture was entitled "Every Woman is a Goddess." Page 58 told Expo attendees that professional astrologer Gregory Bogart was there to give a talk on "Astrology: A Spiritual Awakening." A special "Featured Workshop" was advertised on page 32:

> BETTY EADIE: *Embraced By The Light*. Her death experience is one of the most amazing stories ever told. She will recount in vivid detail what she saw and learned from the other side, what happens when

we die, and the wonderful opportunities we have while we are in our physical bodies.

It was standing room only at Eadie's Saturday, April 23, 1994, workshop. She of course made no mention of her LDS membership. Nor did she advertise herself as a "devout" Christian. Instead, she simply shared her experience, especially the more New Age-sounding aspects of it.

To see exactly how *Embraced By The Light* promotes New Age teachings, a person must first know a little something about the New Age movement and its doctrines. Consequently, the remainder of this chapter will focus on these issues.

Meet the New Age

Although nearly everyone has heard of the New Age movement, not everyone defines it the same way. As Henry Gordon of the Committee for the Scientific Investigation of Claims of the Paranormal (CSICOP) says, "Ask ten sociologists for a definition of the New Age movement, and you may get ten different answers."[4] Gordon continues:

> The New Age encompasses the entire field of the paranormal and all the irrational beliefs associated with it. This smorgasbord includes yoga, mysticism, astrology, acupuncture, chiropractic, nature cults, hypnosis, herbal medicine, Jungian psychology, dietary therapy, meditation, faith healing, telepathy, psychokinesis, spiritualism, clairvoyance, biofeedback, biorhythms, reincarnation, and all sorts of psychological techniques for "heightened awareness."[5]

Award-winning journalist and religion writer Russell Chandler has characterized the New Age movement as a "hybrid mix of spiritual, social, and political forces, and it encompasses sociology, theology, the physical sciences, medicine, anthropology, history, the human potential movement, sports, and science fiction."[6]

J. Gordon Melton, a nationally recognized chronicler of religions, has gone so far as to call it an international social and religious movement which has shown itself to be "an important new force in the development of the ever-changing Western culture."[7]

The New Age movement requires such wordy descriptions because it is more than just an isolated system of religious beliefs and practices. It is literally a *movement* comprised of countless spiritually oriented groups seeking to direct the path of society. Adding to the movement's complexity is the fact that these groups, while having many beliefs in common, often hold to numerous doctrinal distinctives. At times they may even disagree with each other on significant issues.

New Agers, despite their many differences, all seem to share a clear goal: get New Age beliefs into every aspect of society. This, for all intents and purposes, has already been accomplished. Through organized rallies, huge conventions, free literature and high profile personalities like actress Shirley MacLaine, New Age philosophies have infiltrated the entertainment industry, the food industry, public school curricula, health care services, the political arena, the business world and even the United States military.

The term "New Age" is applied to this movement because those involved in it believe that humanity is about to make an evolutionary leap of man's spiritual nature which will eventually bring about the "emergence of a new cycle of human consciousness and experience . . . ."[8]

This coming *new* age will be marked by global peace, mass enlightenment, and unparalleled spiritual advancement. Even now the earth is allegedly being made ready for a final "transformation from out-moded habits, negative energies and thought forms . . . ."[9]

One of these out-moded thought forms is the Christian concept of God. New Age spokesperson Marilyn Ferguson admits that in "the emergent spiritual tradition [i.e., the New Age movement] God is not the personage of our Sunday school mentality . . . ."[10] What kind of god does this "emergent spiritual tradition" preach? The answer to that question will be the first stop on our brief tour through the New Age movement.

Winds of the East

To most New Agers, God is an impersonal force permeating "all that is." This view flows naturally from the New Age movement's most foundational belief—monism, which literally means "one." It teaches that all is one and one is all. *Every* New Ager believes that there ultimately exists only one cosmic substance. The diversity we perceive is actually unreal. It is all an illusion. As New Ager David Spangler puts it: "Oneness is the only reality and diversity is its apparent manifestation."[11]

In other words, people only *think* that a rock lying in a field is something entirely separate from the field in which it is lying. The reality is that the rock *is* the field, and the field *is* the rock. Similarly, people only *think* that they are individual entities. The reality is that there is no "you-me" distinction. There is only one big "I."

This "I" includes not just every *person*, but also every *thing* (e.g., sand, books, seashells, asphalt, etc.). Everyone is everything; everything is everyone. All things that exist are merely different manifestations of the one universal substance usually referred to by New Agers as the Reality, Power, All, Mind, Force, Absolute, Principle or Energy. The most sought-after state of consciousness is one in which "all individuality dissolves into universal, undifferentiated oneness."[12]

Monism is foundational not only to the New Age movement, but also to Hinduism. Hindu literature is saturated with it. For example, a family of Hindu scriptures known as the Upanishads read:

> There are, assuredly, two forms of Brahma [the one reality]: the formed and the formless. Now, that which is the formed is unreal; that which is the formless is real . . . .[13]
>
> [T]his whole world is Brahma. Tranquil, let one worship It as that from which he came forth, as that into which he will be dissolved, as that in which he breathes.[14]

A monistic world view is often accompanied by a doctrine known as pantheism, which asserts that everything is "God." New Agers reason: If everything that exists is one, and "God" is part of all that exists, then "God" must also be one with everything that is. This, again, is Hinduism.

In many ways the New Age movement is little more than Hinduism disguised in Western terminology and presented as a new brand of spirituality which will prove to be mankind's long-awaited key to Utopia. The only substantive difference between Hinduism and the New Age movement is that Hinduism is world-*denying* while the New Age movement is world-*affirming*. The asceticism of India's primary religion has been replaced by something much more palatable to American tastebuds—materialism.

In opposition to the New Age movement's Hinduistic philosophy is the Bible, which reveals that God is not all and all is not God. Genesis 1:1, "In the beginning God created the heavens and the earth," clearly portrays God as an entity who is separate and distinct from the universe. The entire first chapter of Genesis systematically shows that God, rather than being a *part* of all that exists, is the *Creator* of all that exists. This is demonstrated in many other biblical passages including Isaiah 40:22, 42:5, Jeremiah 27:5 and Acts 17:23-24.

God is also not an impersonal Substance or Cosmic Force. In Exodus 3:13-15, the Lord applies to Himself the divine name "I [first person singular] AM [the verb *to be*]." Only someone with a personal knowledge of "self" can say "I AM." Consequently, God must be a person.

Furthermore, God performs acts which are only attributable to a personal being. In Jeremiah 29:11, He declares that He knows the plans that He has for His people. How can an impersonal force know something or have plans? God hears (Exodus 2:24), sees (Hebrews 4:13), speaks (Leviticus 19:1), knows all things (1 John 3:20) and loves (Proverbs 3:12; Jeremiah 31:3).

In sharp contrast to the impersonal god of the New Age movement, the God of Christianity is an intelligent, compassionate and personal being. He is the *living* God (1 Timothy 3:15, 4:10; Hebrews 3:12, 10:31), and the *true* God (2 Chronicles 15:3; Jeremiah 10:10; 1 Thessalonians 1:9). As such, He is also the quintessential enemy of New Agers whose most cherished belief is that *they* are God.

"I Am God"

Belief in monism and pantheism is what leads New Agers into believing that they are God. The relationship between these three concepts—monism, pantheism and man's divinity—is articulated well in "Teddy," J.D. Salinger's short story about a spiritually precocious boy who at 10 years old became "enlightened" while watching his little sister drink milk:

> I was six when I saw that everything was God. . . .
> My sister was only a very tiny child then, and she was drinking her milk, and all of a sudden I saw that *she* was God and the *milk* was God. I mean, all she was doing was pouring God into God . . . . [15]

Shirley MacLaine (dancer, actress, film star), who became "a major voice in the New Age community following the publication of her book, *Out on a Limb*, and the television dramatization of the book,"[16] has made some of the most explicit and widely heard New Age proclamations of self-realized godhood. During one scene in her five-hour television adaptation of *Out on a Limb*, MacLaine unabashedly proclaims "I AM GOD! I AM GOD!"

In a book produced after *Out on a Limb*, MacLaine attempts to give her fans a deeper understanding of the reasoning behind her belief: "I *know* that I exist, therefore I AM. I *know* that the God-source exists. Therefore IT IS. Since I am part of that force, then I AM that I AM."[17]

New Agers, rather than accusing MacLaine of blasphemy, congratulate her for obtaining that which all of us should be striving to achieve—"enlightenment." The Bible, on the other hand, consistently draws a distinction between God and man. Passages such as Psalm 33:13–15, 100:3, Ecclesiastes 5:2, Isaiah 43:7 and Malachi 2:10 make it very plain that God is utterly distinct from man.

It can additionally be demonstrated from Romans 1:25 that man is not God. In this verse, Paul the apostle mentions those who exchange the truth of God for a lie so that they can worship and serve the creature rather than the Creator. Christian author Eldon K. Winker points out in *The New Age Is Lying to You* that worship of the creature is possible only if the creature is distinct and separate from the Creator.[18]

In *The Counterfeit Christ of the New Age Movement*, New Age critic Ron Rhodes makes a series of comparisons which also show the various dissimilarities between God and man:

> God is all-knowing (Is. 40:13–14), but man is limited in knowledge (Job 38:4); God is all-powerful (Rev. 19:6), but man is weak (Heb. 4:15); God is everywhere-present (Ps. 139:7–12), but man is confined to a single space at a time (John 1:50); God is holy (1 John 1:5), but even man's "righteous" deeds are as filthy garments before God (Is. 64:6); God is eternal (Ps. 90:2), but man was created at a point in time (Gen. 1:1, 26–27). . . . God is characterized by justice (Acts 17:31), but man is lawless (1 John 3:4; see also Rom. 3:23).[19]

Don't Say the "H" Word

In the New Age movement, everyone will be saved via absorption back into the ultimate One (sometimes referred to as going to heaven). New Agers find the Christian concept of hell repulsive, to say the least. Some believe that nearly all of the world's problems are due to the idea of a transcendent God who will judge people for their sins:

> [T]wo-thirds of evil (for humanity) comes from false God concepts, promoted by clever minds to enslave humanity. There is no God, no one intelligent entity outside His creation . . . .[20]

To New Agers, it is unconscionable that any individual could be separated from God for eternity. After all, everyone is *already* one with God. We need only to realize our oneness more and more until, through successive lifetimes (reincarnation), we merge back into that great One from which we came.

Benjamin Creme, a well-known New Age author, assures everyone that the path to God is "broad enough to take in all men."[21] Jesus, however, said that the way to God is narrow. The broad way, according to our Lord, is the way "that leads to destruction, and many enter through it" (Matthew 7:13).

Jesus' comment typifies the kind of "intolerant" and "narrow-minded" thinking that New Agers hope will fade from existence as their era of universal harmony dawns. There is no room for those who believe in only one Savior. In the New Age, all religions are equally valid and all religious leaders are of equal worth: Buddha, Mohammed, Zoroaster, Confucius, Krishna, Jesus, whoever.

The importance of each leader lies in what he or she taught, rather than in his or her personal identity. When it comes right down to it (for a New Ager), whether or not a "great teacher" ever *really* existed is relatively unimportant. Only his or her teachings (or someone's teachings) are necessary. The teacher's words, rather than his or her life, are what help individuals reach a state of peace and harmony with the universe.

This is the great difference between Christianity and other religions. The Christian faith is founded upon a Person, Jesus Christ, God in the flesh. Not only do His teachings have meaning in and of themselves, but they are backed by His identity and exemplary life. A Christian's faith would be in vain if Jesus had not accomplished what He came to earth to do: to die for our sins and rise again from the dead (1 Corinthians 15:14). It is through Christ's resurrection life that new life is imparted to those who place their trust in Him (2 Timothy 2:11–12).

New Age doctrines are designed to do one thing—lead people away from Christianity. This is now occurring through *Embraced By The Light*. The apostle Paul warned that in the later times some would "fall away from the faith, paying attention to deceitful spirits and doctrines of demons" (1 Timothy 4:1). Paul was right.

ENDNOTES

[1] Miller, Elliot. *A Crash Course on the New Age Movement*, p. 186.

[2] n.a. *1994 Whole Life Expo Program Guide*, "Imagine A World of Possibilities," p. 27.

[3] Ibid., p. 3.

[4] Gordon, Henry. *Channeling into the New Age*, p. 21.

[5] Ibid.

[6] Chandler, Russell. *Understanding the New Age*, p. 17

[7] Melton, J. Gordon. *New Age Encyclopedia*, p. xiii.

[8] Spangler, David. *Revelation: The Birth of A New Age*, p. 19.

[9] Ingenito, Marcia Gervase. *National New Age Yellow Pages*, 1987 edition, "Colors & New Age Transformation" by Elizabeth Long, D.D., p. 61.

[10] Ferguson, Marilyn. *The Aquarian Conspiracy*, p. 382.

[11] Spangler, op. cit., p. 194.

[12] Capra, Fritjof. *Turning Point: Science, Society, and the Rising Culture*, p. 371.

[13] Hume, Robert, Ernest, translator. *The Thirteen Principal Upanishads*, "Maitri Upanishad," 6.3, p. 425.

[14] Ibid., "Chandogya Upanishad," 3.14.1, p. 209.

[15] Salinger, J.D. *Nine Stories*, p. 288.

[16] Melton, op. cit., p. 270.

[17] MacLaine, Shirley. *Dancing in the Light*, p. 420.

[18] Winkler, Eldon, K. *The New Age Is Lying to You*, p. 191.

[19] Rhodes, Ron. *The Counterfeit Christ of the New Age Movement*, p. 161.

[20] Two Disciples. *The Rainbow Bridge*, p. 13.

[21] Creme, Benjamin. *The Reappearance of the Christ and the Masters of Wisdom*, p. 120.

CHAPTER 6

Betty Eadie:
Newest New Age Guru

Where does Charisma *[& Christian Life magazine] get off reporting that Betty J. Eadie's* Embraced By The Light *promotes "New Age-style beliefs?". . . Nowhere in the book does she present any idea that might contradict New Testament Christianity.*

— Dennis R. Holt, Christian[1]

Betty Eadie, as we have seen, is not a devout Christian. But neither can she be considered a devout Mormon. *Embraced By The Light* advances New Age doctrines which directly conflict with Mormon theology. This may sound problematic, but it has actually proven to be a great marketing plus.

Embraced By The Light appeals to nearly everyone. Mormons are flocking to Eadie's side for obvious reasons. Christians are being drawn to her book merely because of some evangelical-sounding phrases which she has coupled with the name "Jesus." Now, New Agers are getting into the act because Eadie has managed to put an ever-so-subtle gloss of New Age terminology over her Mormon and pseudo-Christian beliefs.

In the previous chapter we looked at various New Age doctrines: 1) all is one and one is all (Monism); 2) all is God

(Pantheism); 3) man is God; 4) there is no hell; and 5) all religions are equally valid. What needs to now be discerned is whether or not Eadie puts forth any of these teachings.

Mormonism to Monism

Several remarks by Eadie suggest, at least to New Agers, that she believes all is one, God is all, and we are God. She has not spoken or written extensively on these doctrines, but has simply made enough monistic/pantheistic comments to make New Agers comfortable:

New Age Movement	Betty Eadie
[I]n the Eastern religions and philosophies. . . . This relationship simply affirms that *all life is one* . . . (emphasis added).[2]	I felt God in the plant, in me, his love pouring into us. *We were all one* (emphasis added).[6]
The universal God is one, yet he is more than one; all things are God; *all things are one* (emphasis added).[3]	*[B]eing one with everything else* was so great that I will cherish it forever (emphasis added).[7]
The inner reality is man's Oneness, a shared *divine nature* which is potential in every single human being . . . (emphasis added).[4]	[W]e are all *divine by nature* (emphasis added).[8]
Each one of us is a part of that spirit—*a divine entity* (emphasis added).[5]	*Each and every one of us is divine . . .*" (emphasis added).[9]

Eadie is technically contradicting her LDS theology here. But she is also taking Mormonism out to its logical conclusion. Remember, Mormons believe that everything, including God, is made out of the same eternal "substance" (intelligence) which has been organized into its present form. If one were able to go far enough back in time, "all that is" would be part of this same universal substance. What we now see are the manifestations of that "intelligence" (eternal spirit, self-existent matter, etc.). An early Mormon scholar put it this way:

> This spirit which pervades all things. . . . is the spirit of intelligence. . . . If you see a living blade of grass you see a manifestation of that Spirit which is called God. If you see an animal of any kind on the face of the earth having life, there is a manifestation of that Spirit. If you see a man you behold its most perfect earthly manifestation. And if you see a glorified man [God]. . . . He is a perfect manifestation, expression and revelation of this eternal essence, this spirit of eternal, everlasting intelligence [10] . . . .

This Mormonized version of monism/pantheism appears on pages 79–80 of *Embraced By The Light*. The scene is a heavenly garden:

> [E]ach part of the plant, each microscopic part, is made up of its own *intelligence*. . . . Every minute part is filled with its own life and can be reorganized with other elements to create anything in existence . . . . it has *intelligence* and organization . . . . Life. It was in the water too. Each drop from the waterfall had its own *intelligence* . . . (emphasis added).

Consider the following excerpt taken from *Revelation: The Birth of A New Age* by David Spangler:

> [I]t has been known by mystics and pioneers of advanced consciousness throughout the centuries that all the universe is alive and everything is the manifestation of some form of living *Intelligence*. Now, as part of the revelations of the New Age, this knowledge is being spread more widely (emphasis

added).[11]

Spangler's reference to "intelligence" is common among New Agers. Sun Bear, medicine chief of the Bear Tribe Medicine Society, also mentions "intelligences in the universe that help the healer" which may be called "God, the Great Spirit, Spirit Helpers, or whatever."[12]

For Mormons, "intelligence" conjures up images of preexistence. New Agers, on the other hand, hear monism/pantheism in the word. To say that the coincidence has been beneficial for Betty Eadie is an understatement.

All Roads Lead to God

New Agers, although opposed to Christian "narrow-mindedness," will often purchase Christian-sounding literature as long as it allows for acceptance of other religious beliefs. This attitude relates to another New Age concept advanced by Eadie—all religions are equally important and needed:

New Age Movement	Embraced By The Light
[I]t matters not which world religion you follow if it takes you to God with clarity and certainty that death is not the end.[13]	People in one religion may not have a complete understanding of the Lord's gospel and never will have while in that religion. But that religion is used as a stepping stone to further knowledge (p. 45).
[T]he teachings of Christ as we [New Agers] know them are meant for people of a higher level than we ourselves. And the lost element in Christianity is the specific	Each of us, I was told, is at a different level of spiritual development and understanding. Each person is therefore prepared for a different level of spiritual knowledge. . . .

(continued on next page)

New Age Movement	Embraced By The Light
methods and ideas that can . . . lead us toward the level at which the teachings of Christ can be followed. . . . there are levels in Christianity.[14]	Each church fulfills spiritual needs that perhaps others cannot fill. No one church can fulfill everybody's needs at every level (p. 45).
Let us have unity about our love for God within the diversity of the various groups and not separate ourselves as superior or more beloved than others.[15]	[W]e have no right to criticize any church or religion in any way. They are all precious and important in his [God's] sight (p. 46).

New Teachings for an Awakening Humanity, a book allegedly written by "the Christ," reads: *"God is assisting mankind's return home in an evolving progress one step at a time."*[16] Note the similarity between this "channeled" statement and Eadie's dialogue with Oprah Winfrey.[17]

OPRAH We're all evolving to get back home?
BETTY Exactly. That's it.

In order to be sure I understood Eadie's view about world religions, I asked her about teachers like Zoroaster and Buddha as well as all the other gods who are worshiped. Her answer was textbook New Age:[18]

EADIE I think we are all believing in the same God. I think that we just have had different instructors, or different leaders, you might say.
ABANES In your book you say that Jesus was God. Is that correct?
EADIE [pause] He was the God of earth. He was helping the creation of earth.
ABANES Is there a God above him, so to speak, that we—
EADIE [interrupting] His Father. Our Father.

ABANES That is "the Light" that all of us believe in, but have different teachers about?
EADIE Right!

Eadie obviously contradicted herself in the above discussion by saying that "the Light" was the Father when previously she had stated that "the Light" was Jesus Christ. More important to our present discussion, however, is her expressed agreement with the classic New Age belief that all religions worship the same God despite conflicting beliefs. *The Aquarian Gospel of Jesus Christ*, produced by occultist Levi H. Dowling, matches Eadie's view:

> All people worship God, the One; but all people see him not alike. . . . The nations of the earth see God from different points of view, and so he does not seem the same to everyone.[19]

Because everyone is worshiping the same God, says Eadie, all religions upon the earth "are necessary because there are people who need what they teach."[20] This certainly sounds appealing and "loving," but what about the false doctrines in many religions? Scripture says false doctrines should be condemned (Jude 3).

What about harmful religions? Charles Manson invented a self-styled religion that taught plenty. How much of *it* was needed? David Koresh had a great deal to teach as well, especially to pre-pubescent girls. There was also Jim Jones. How about the neo-Nazi/White Supremacist groups within the "Christian Identity" movement which teach that Jews have "the sly characteristics of the serpent"[21] and view the white race as superior? One well-known Identity teacher, in reference to training his children about interracial marriage, states: "I teach them also that if they ever did such a thing never to come around my house with their mate or their half-breed children because they've been traitors to their own sires."[22]

Eadie allegedly received her revelations about the world's religions after asking Jesus why God did not "give us only one church, one pure religion?"[23] Her question could have been answered with Scripture.

The apostle Peter preached: "There is salvation in no one else; for there is no other name under heaven that has been given among men, by which we must be saved" (Acts 4:12). Paul wrote: "There is *one* mediator between God and men, the man Christ Jesus" (1 Timothy 2:5). There *is* one true religion—Christianity.

Statements like these, however, can be distasteful to many. Some could even be offended by Eadie's identification of "the Light" as being Jesus Christ. An obvious solution would be to have a more acceptable answer ready. On "The Oprah Winfrey Show" Eadie provided just such an answer. She told the celebrity talk show host that the identity of the light depended on one's religious upbringing. This, despite the fact that Eadie had previously said the "Light" was definitely Jesus:

Betty Eadie	"The Oprah Winfrey Show"[28]
I ran to this being, and as I ran to him it was very clear to me that he was Jesus Christ. There is absolutely no doubt in my mind who he was.[24]	*OPRAH* Now do you think. . . . it was Jesus Christ because in your religious training that is what you knew the light to be? And so, perhaps maybe if you were of another religious background— [interrupted by Betty]
There was no questioning who he was. I knew that he was my Savior, and friend, and God. He was Jesus Christ . . . .[25]	*BETTY* They might see their religious leader.
As I approached that light, that is when I realized who that light was . . . . I knew that he was Jesus Christ.[26]	*OPRAH* As Buddha, for instance?

BETTY Yes. They might see their religious leader. Yes. |

(continued on next page)

Betty Eadie	"The Oprah Winfrey Show"
[The Light was] my Lord and Savior Jesus Christ. . . . It would be easy if I wanted to be popular; I could have left Him as just a being of light. But I had to tell it as it is . . . .[27]	OPRAH But whatever the title given, it was emanating such love and light. BETTY That's right.

During an interview with *The Arizona Republic*, Eadie again seemed to vacillate on the identity of the light when she said, "For me, it was Jesus, but it didn't seem to matter to him what you called him."[29]

More contradictory statements surfaced during an interview with Hugh Downs on ABC's "20/20" program. Downs asked Eadie an extremely important question about our identities, personalities, life accomplishments and positions in the world, which, according to Eadie, we all chose during our premortal existence. Her response was the exact opposite of what she had written in her runaway bestseller. Given the question asked, it is easy to see why she would do such a thing:

Embraced By The Light	"20/20"[30]
[I]n the pre-mortal world we knew about and *even chose our missions in life* . . . Our stations in life are based upon the objectives of those missions (p. 48, emphasis added).	HUGH Why would a spirit choose to come to earth maybe only to become a Hitler or a Stalin or a Charles Manson?

(continued on next page)

Embraced By The Light	"20/20"
[W]e all *volunteered for our positions* and stations in the world. . . . *We also chose* to come to earth with certain others because of the work we would do together. . . . we could best do it with certain circumstances brought about by *selected parents or others* (pp. 53, 92–93, emphasis added).	BETTY I don't think they necessarily chose to be that particular person. Circumstances in their life, perhaps a dysfunction in their family brought them to a point of total dysfunction themselves.

Eadie's appearance with Oprah was much less confrontational. The well-known talk show host seemed to agree with Eadie on everything.[31]

OPRAH I believe that there are many paths to God.
BETTY Yes.
OPRAH Or, many paths to the light. I certainly don't believe that there is only one way. . . . Did Jesus indicate that to you?
BETTY Yes, absolutely. . . . Every church was saying that they are the only one, and now I was experiencing something that was absolutely different than I had been taught in any of the churches.
OPRAH Well, I'm glad to hear that because if Jesus is as cool as I think He is, he would have had to tell you that.
BETTY He was, He was. . . . He said about the other faiths that it didn't really matter. That love was the ultimate. That if we loved one another, that everything else would be okay. That not one church could be there for every person. That we're all unique. That we're at various levels of spiritual development. Not only here on earth, but there as well. So, that is what's most important is just loving one another.

Jesus Christ may not be as "cool" as Betty and Oprah

believe Him to be. In John 14:6, He says: "I am the way and the truth and the life. No one comes to the Father except through me." Jesus also warns, "The man who does not enter the sheep pen by the gate, but climbs in by some other way, is a thief and a robber. . . .I am the gate; whoever enters through me will be saved. He will come in and go out, and find pasture" (John 10:1, 9).

If I Should Die Before I Wake...

Like most New Agers, Eadie feels that every single person will be saved. Her only qualifier—sometimes—is that it will be through Jesus. "Whether we learn of Jesus Christ here or while in the spirit [after we die]," she asserts, "we must eventually accept him and surrender to his love."[32] Even atheists, according to Eadie, will have the opportunity to accept Jesus after they die.[33]

At one of her lectures she read a question someone had submitted to her: "Is everyone allowed in heaven?" Her answer was as straightforward as the question: "Yes."[34] When I spoke with Eadie in January of 1994, she told me the same thing, but clarified, "That doesn't mean we all return there [heaven] immediately."

"Maybe aeons and aeons in the future?" I inquired.

"Oh, yes. I believe that."

Exactly how atheists and other nonchristians move on toward accepting "Jesus" after death depends upon what *they* want to do:

When we "die" . . . we experience nothing more than a transition. . . . we are given the choice to remain on earth until our bodies are buried or to move on. . . . there are many levels of development, and we will always go to that level where we are most comfortable. . . . those who have bonded to the world through greed, bodily appetites, or other earthly commitments . . . become earth-bound. . . . These spirits stay on the earth. . . . They reside there as long as they want to . . . eventually they learn to move on to accept the greater warmth and security of God.[35]

Eadie says, "God is so loving, so gentle, that if you die in darkness—if you die in disbelief—he will not startle your belief system by taking you immediately from that to Him, but rather, allow you to progress gradually as you can."[36]

Scripture says nothing about spirits lingering on earth after death or about proceeding on to levels of spiritual development where one is most comfortable. Neither does the Bible mention anything about having after-death choices to move on at one's own pace. It also contains no verses about God not wanting to "shock" erroneous belief systems. God's Word tells us that it is appointed for men to die once and *after this* comes judgment (Hebrews 9:27).

Those who have received Christ as their personal Savior will immediately be at home with the Lord (Philippians 1:21–23; 2 Corinthians 5:8). Individuals who have not come to a saving knowledge of Christ during this lifetime will first go to an intermediate state of punishment where they will await a *final* judgment (Job 21:30–34; Isaiah 14:9–11). Second Peter 2:9 says "If this is so, then the Lord knows how to rescue godly men from trials and to hold the unrighteous for the day of judgment, while continuing their punishment." At the final judgment they will be told to depart from God's presence (Matthew 7:23) into what Scripture terms the Lake of Fire (Revelation 20:10–14). In short, *now* is the day of salvation (2 Corinthians 6:2).

Eadie, on the other hand, says there is no future judgment. A post-death "life review" is about the only thing we will have to face. And to make things even easier on us, *we* will do the judging rather than God. Even then, she says, Jesus will make sure we are not too hard on ourselves:

> I stepped to my left to watch the review. . . . I saw the disappointment that I had caused others. . . . all the suffering I had caused, and felt it. . . . I saw how much grief my bad temper had caused, and I suffered this grief. I saw my selfishness. . . . Everything about me was taken into consideration, how I was raised, the things I had been taught. . . . the council [spirit beings with her] was *not judging me*. I was judging myself. . . . The Savior stepped toward me. . . . he said that I was judging myself too critically. "You're being

too harsh on yourself," he said.[37]

While on "The Oprah Winfrey Show," Eadie added that hell is simply the momentary suffering that is felt when, during a life review, we realize the grief that we have caused others:

BETTY I had always felt that God would judge me. Being the judgmental God that I was taught that He was. But I understood that we actually store everything in our brain and we judge ourself. I was shown from the very beginning of my life the negative things that I had done, pain that I had created for another person. . . . No one sat in judgment of me. When you go through your life review you re-experience the pain you have caused someone else—that's the hell that I felt.
OPRAH That in itself is the judgment?
BETTY Yes.

New Agers, like Eadie, reject the idea of a transcendent God who will judge:

New Age Movement	Betty Eadie
[T]he Christ is a very simple man, and is not a judge.[38]	I felt no judgment for having been mistaken [about doctrine].[42]
God has never judged you or anyone.[39]	No one sat in judgment of me.[43]
[God] never made a hell; we are creators and we make our own.[40]	If you're bad on earth, generally you punish yourself.[44]
. . . God; how great this Entity-Self is . . . that will allow you to be and do anything you wish and hold you judgeless.[41]	. . . I had always felt that God would judge me. . . . we judge ourselves.[45]

What about sin? According to Eadie, we ignorantly view sin as something bad when it is ultimately something good. Sins, although they may cause a few temporary negative feelings, present chances for growth. "In the spirit world they don't see sin as we do here," Eadie promises. "*All experiences can be positive. All are learning experiences.*"[46] She continues: "I saw my sins and short-comings in a multi-dimensional light. Yes, they were grievous to me and others, but they were tools for me to learn by."[47]

Eadie holds this view of sin because she maintains that sin is going against impersonal laws of the universe—like gravity: "I saw that there are many laws by which we are governed—spiritual laws, physical laws, and universal laws . . . . When we break one of these laws, going against that which is the natural order, we have sinned."[48] During a 1994 radio interview, she gave an example of sin:

> When we hear "sin" we cringe. But actually you create a sin when you take a glass and hold it over a cement floor and you release the glass. That is a sin because you have broken the law of gravity. But you would not feel that you are condemned to hell because you did it.[49]

Downplaying the seriousness of sin is especially appealing to New Agers who look to no moral standard and want nothing to do with an objective code of righteousness. New Agers decide for themselves what is right because they are God:

> . . . God is everything—He is every *thing*. So *any* thing you do, you have an inner action in divinity. Remember that, and do what you want to do . . . .[50]

Anything is permissible for most New Agers not only because they are God, but also because sin and evil are unreal to them. Like everything else, sin/evil and good/righteousness are illusions. Everything is one. That which is termed "evil" is merely "the manifestation of a force that is out of place or out of timing, inappropriate to the needs and realities of the situation."[51]

Many New Agers contradict themselves on this point. They maintain that there is no good or evil, only the great Absolute (i.e., the single Substance which constitutes all reality), but at the same time assert that there are indeed some things which are inherently "good" (e.g., ecology, health food, animal rights) and "bad" (intolerance of other religions). Apparently, the no-distinction-between-good-and-evil rule only applies when discussing the judgment of a transcendent God.

A few New Agers, like Benjamin Creme, pursue their monism to its logical end and do not hesitate to say that the forces of evil are actually "part of God." According to Creme, evil forces "are not separate from God. Everything is God. There is nothing else in fact but God."[52]

Closely linked to the issue of sin is the issue of forgiveness. To Eadie and New Agers, forgiveness comes from within. Once we forgive ourselves, all we need do is go on and try harder next time. "God" need not forgive us because He unconditionally accepts and loves us exactly as we are. Sin only makes "God" sad because it makes *us* sad, and when we are sad we cannot progress along our paths of experience at optimum speed. "We need to forgive ourselves," realizes Eadie, "and be grateful for the things that help us grow."[53]

New Age Movement	*Embraced By The Light*
[W]hen you can *forgive yourself* and *allow the love of that Omnipresent Essence* to become a part of you. That is what individualizes you (emphasis added).[54]	If I had broken laws or sinned, I needed to change my heart, *forgive myself*, and then move onward. . . . I needed to approach God and *feel his love again*—his healing love (pp. 69–70, emphasis added).

(continued on next page)

New Age Movement	Embraced By The Light
If people *know* God loves them, that creates happiness in people. It doesn't matter if they love Him; *it doesn't matter how they think they've been in their life* or how they are, because how they are isn't important; if they *know* that *God is going to love them regardless* . . . (emphasis added).[55]	I knew that he [Jesus] was aware of *all my sins and faults, but that they didn't matter right now.* He just wanted to hold me and *share his love with me* . . . (pp. 41–42, emphasis added).

When it comes to sin, forgiveness and judgment, New Agers look upon orthodox Christianity as the epitome of all that belongs to the unenlightened, discardable and patently offensive "old" age which must soon pass away. Take, for instance, the following New Age sentiments, which one can only assume are shared by Eadie:

> [F]or two thousand years, we have been called *sinful creatures*. That stigma automatically takes away our ability to remind ourselves that we are great, or that we are equal with God or Christ or Buddha, or whomever.[56]
> The Christian religion is replete with guilt and negativity and needs to be changed.[57]

Another Point of View

The biblical definition of sin and Eadie's definition of sin are vastly different. Sin, according to Scripture, is any action or thought contrary to God's expressed will (James 4:12, 17). Furthermore, the Law that sin breaks is a moral Law proceeding from a personal God (1 John 3:4), not an impersonal law of an impersonal universe.

According to Isaiah 59:2, sins create a "separation" between man and God, which is why the prayers of unbelievers are not heard by the Lord. The separation can only be bridged by Christ. Only through Him does someone have access to God (1 Timothy 2:5). *Embraced By The Light*, on the other hand, declares that people are never separated from God (p. 41) and that everyone's prayers are automatically heard (p. 104).

Concerning forgiveness for sin, it does not come from within oneself, but rather from God (Exodus 34:7; Psalm 130:4; Luke 23:34). First John 1:9 says, "If we confess our sins, he is faithful and just and will forgive us our sins and purify us from all unrighteousness." This forgiveness can only be obtained through personal faith in Jesus Christ (Matthew 26:28; Acts 5:31–32, 10:43; Ephesians 4:32; 1 John 2:12).

Those who do not receive forgiveness will receive judgment (Acts 24:25; Ephesians 5:6; Romans 2:5; 1 Corinthians 11:32; Colossians 3:6; 1 Thessalonians 1:7–10), and God will be the one who judges (Romans 2:16, 14:10; Hebrews 13:4; James 4:12). In fact, all judgment has been given to the Son (John 5:22; Acts 10:42; 2 Corinthians 5:10) and only those who are in Christ will escape His wrath. John 5:24 says, "I tell you the truth, whoever hears my word and believes him who sent me has eternal life and will not be condemned; he has crossed over from death to life." (See also Romans 8:1).

Regarding Eadies post-death "life-review," there are absolutely no Scriptural verses that refer to such an option during which all of us will suffer a "hell" via the re-experiencing of the pain we have caused others. Eadie's "life-review" concept comes not from the Bible, but entirely from her NDE.

Eadie promotes many other New Age ideas including universal energies, positive/negative vibrations, mind power, reality creating, and self-healing. These, too, as the following chapter will show, are in opposition to Scripture.

ENDNOTES

[1] Holt, Dennis R. *Charisma & Christian Life*, "Letters to the Editor," July 1994, p. 10.

[2] Spangler, David. *Revelation: The Birth of A New Age*, p. 233.

[3] Dowling, Levi H. *The Aquarian Gospel of Jesus the Christ*, 28:4, p. 64.

[4] Creme, Benjamin. *Maitreya's Mission*, p. 107.

[5] Gawain, Shakti. *Living in the Light*, p. 35.

[6] Eadie, Betty. *Embraced By The Light*, p. 81.

[7] Ibid.

[8] Eadie, Betty. Taped seminar as aired by "20/20" program on ABC, 5/13/94.

[9] Ibid.

[10] Penrose, Charles W. *Journal of Discourses*, 26:23–24, "Discourse delivered by Elder Charles W. Penrose, Delivered in the Tabernacle, Salt Lake City, Sunday Afternoon, November 16, 1884."

[11] Spangler, op. cit., p. 109.

[12] Carlson, Richard and Benjamin Shield, eds. *Healers on Healing*, "Healing Attitudes" by Sun Bear, p. 151.

[13] Essene, Virginia. *New Teachings for an Awakening Humanity*, p. 116.

[14] Needleman, Jacob. *Lost Christianity*, p. 155 as quoted in *The Cosmic Self* by Ted Peters, p. 119.

[15] Essene, op. cit.

[16] Ibid., p. 124.

[17] "The Oprah Winfrey Show," 1/3/94 (re-aired 8/3/94).

[18] Eadie, Betty. Author's 1/25/94 interview with Eadie.

[19] Dowling, op. cit., 28:13, 17, p. 65.

[20] Eadie, *Embraced*, p. 45.

[21] Mohr, Jack. "Seed of Satan: Literal or Figurative?" p. 26 as quoted in *Christian Research Journal*, "Identity: A Christian Religion for White Racists" by Viola Larson, Fall 1992, p. 23.

[22] Peters, Pete. *Inter-Racial Marriage*, part 1 (cassette 170) as quoted in *Christian Research Journal*, "Identity: A Christian Religion for White Racists" by Viola Larson, Fall 1992, p. 25.

[23] Eadie, *Embraced*, p. 45.

[24] Eadie, Betty. WMUZ 3/3/94 interview with Al Kresta.

[25] Eadie, *Embraced*, p. 42.

[26] Eadie, Betty. "20/20" program on ABC, 5/13/94.

27 Miller, Leslie. *USA Today*, "Betty Eadie, Shedding 'Light' On Her Visit to Heaven," 8/12/93, p. 5D.

28 "The Oprah Winfrey Show," op. cit.

29 Price, Kathie. *The Arizona Republic*, "Visiting Death: Woman Tells of Glimpse of Paradise," 3/13/93, p. B7.

30 "20/20" program on ABC, 5/13/94.

31 "The Oprah Winfrey Show," op. cit.

32 Eadie, *Embraced*, p. 85.

33 Ibid., pp. 84–85.

34 Eadie, Betty. Taped seminar as aired by "20/20" on ABC, 5/13/94.

35 Eadie, *Embraced*, pp. 83–85.

36 Eadie, WMUZ, op. cit.

37 Eadie, *Embraced*, pp. 112–113.

38 Creme, *The Reappearance of the Christ and the Masters of Wisdom*, p. 120.

39 "Ramtha" with Douglas James Mahr. *Voyage to the New World*, p. 61.

40 Dowling, op. cit., 33:9, p. 71.

41 "Ramtha," op. cit.

42 Eadie, *Embraced*, p. 43.

43 "The Oprah Winfrey Show," op. cit.

44 Eadie, Betty. KGO 810 radio interview as aired by "20/20" program on ABC, 5/13/94.

45 "The Oprah Winfrey Show," op. cit.

46 Eadie, *Embraced*, p. 70.

47 Ibid., pp. 115–116.

48 Ibid., p. 55.

49 Eadie, WMUZ, op. cit.

50 "Ramtha," op. cit., p. 36.

51 Spangler, op. cit., p. 123.

52 Creme, *The Reappearance*, p. 103.

53 Eadie, *Embraced*, p. 71.

54 "Ramtha," op. cit., interview with J.Z. Knight, pp. 179–180.

55 Ibid., p. 179.

56 Ibid., p. 176.

57 Essene, op. cit., p. 81.

CHAPTER 7

Star Wars Theology

The Force, Luke. Use the Force!

— Obi-Wan Kenobi, "Star Wars"

By hour three of my 10 a.m–4 p.m. stay at the 1994 Whole Life Expo, I had spoken to several interesting representatives of the New Age movement: a female channeler dressed in an eight-foot long flowing robe of pink chiffon; members of the Tara Foundation, who say that Christ has returned; a rather rude peddler of miracle-working/cancer-curing spirulina (algae); and an especially jolly fellow offering free weekend trips to his New Age nudist commune in northern California.

I had sought out such encounters in an attempt to understand where these spiritually lost souls were coming from. I asked them a number of questions: Why do you believe that? How do you know that what you believe is true? What is truth? Most of their responses ranged from semi-confused to irrational to self-contradicting. Their sincerity, however, kept up my inquiries.

Around 2 p.m. someone finally asked me a question. As pleased as I was that someone else had initiated a conversation, I was taken rather off guard as I walked along the exhibits.

"Would you like to have your energies aligned?"

"Oh. Uh. Well, I don't . . . "

"They're free!"

I did not know the proper response. I had just finished eating lunch and was unsure as to whether or not my mother's "you-should-never-go-swimming-within-one-hour-of-eating" rule applied to energy alignments. I suddenly blurted out, "No, I'm just looking, thanks."

The moment's pressure, coupled with no time to evaluate the physical demands that energy alignment puts on the body, had caused me to use my standard comeback for retail sales clerks.

A polite, yet somewhat suspicious "OK" from the woman, indicated to me that she knew I had no clear idea of what was going on. I was an "outsider."

Some may consider this an odd encounter, maybe even a bit humorous. But New Agers take their belief in positive and negative energies very seriously. Betty Eadie takes such concepts to heart as well. As she says, "Each spirit has the capacity to be filled with love and eternal energy."[1]

Sheer Energy

Most New Agers believe that there exists an unseen force "running through all of creation and the universe which by many is considered to actually be God. It is something which through various methods can supposedly be controlled for good or bad."[2] *The New Age Almanac* reads:

> Members of the New Age Movement assume the existence of a basic energy that is different from the more recognized forms of energy (heat, light, electromagnetism, gravity, etc.) which supports and permeates all of existence.[3]

Numerous religions throughout the world recognize this energy, or "life force." In Japan it is known as "ki." The Hawaiians and Polynesians call it "mana." To American Indians it is "orenda" and the Hindus of India refer to it as "prana."

Modern practitioners of New Age alternatives to traditional health care have come up with their own labels for it including "the innate" (D.D. Palmer, founder of Chiropractic

Care) and the "vital force" (S. Hahnemann, founder of homeopathy).

Cult researchers John Weldon and Clifford Wilson have observed that there may be as many as "90 different names for the same general energy idea. Although all 90 terms are not fully synonymous, and there is overlap and convergence among them, the basic idea of unusual, unknown energy is central."[4]

The concept of a "life force" seems to have originated in India with Hinduism (3,000 B.C.). To Hindus, this "universal energy residing behind the material world (akasa)"[5] can be a source of tremendous power for those who learn how to master it. A Hindu gains control over "prana" primarily through the kind of breathing techniques (pranayama) that are practiced during yoga:

> What power on earth would not be his? He would be able to move the sun and stars out of their places, to control everything in the universe from the atoms to the biggest suns. This is the end and aim of pranayama. When the yogi becomes perfect there will be nothing in nature not under his control. If he orders the gods or the souls of the departed to come, they will come at his bidding. All the forces of nature will obey him as slaves. . . . He who has controlled prana has controlled his own mind and all the minds . . . and bodies that exist . . . .[6]

The Chinese have a similar view regarding the existence of a mystical energy. They call it "chi." It is foundational to Taoism, one of the three major religions of China (along with Buddhism and Confucianism). Chi is "the energetic force behind all life."[7] It is produced by "the interaction between yin and yang"[8] which are the interacting negative and positive aspects of the universal energy:

> *Chi* circulates through everything in the universe, manifested primarily in its *yin* or *yang* aspect. . . . Although *yin* and *yang* are opposed to each other, ultimately they are still one.[9]

It is Taoist philosophy which most closely resembles what is contained in *Embraced By The Light*. A significant difference exists, however, between Taoism and Eadie's teachings. In Taoism, there is only *one* universal energy with a positive and negative aspect. Eadie maintains there are *two* universal energies; one positive and the other negative.

"Within our universe are both positive and negative energies," Eadie tells us, "and both types of energy are essential to creation and growth."[10] In describing these two energies, Eadie closely parallels the Taoist's explanation of yin and yang:

Taoism	Betty Eadie
Yin is described as that which is *dark*, cold . . . *negative* . . . while yang is described as that which is *light*, warm . . . *positive* . . . . Although yin and yang *are opposite* in nature, it is their ability to interact and balance . . . (emphasis added).[11]	*Positive energy* is basically just what we would think it is: *light*, goodness, . . . and so on. And *negative energy* is just what we would think it is: *darkness*, hatred, . . . and so on. Positive and negative energies work in *opposition* to each other (emphasis added).[12]

Many New Agers feel that certain metaphysical "laws" are closely associated with how this "life force" of the Cosmos works. If one can tap into and obey these laws, then one can control the force. The desired result is power:

New Age Movement	*Embraced By The Light*
Law. . . . is the presence of God's stability and order. . . . the New Age energies cannot abide	[T]here are many laws by which we are governed— spiritual laws, physical laws, and universal laws

(continued on next page)

New Age Movement	Embraced By The Light
where law is broken. . . . Great and *powerful and loving forces have been invoked* and anchored . . . . The patterns of New Age energy may only express themselves through obedience to law . . . (emphasis added).[13]	. . . . When we recognize these laws and learn how to use their positive and negative forces, we will have access to *power beyond comprehension* (p. 55, emphasis added).
The *Law of Cause and Effect* is a part of the experience of everyone. If we make a mistake we suffer the consequences . . . . *if we perform right action, we enjoy the benefits*, in appropriate degrees. . . . As a *Law of Nature*, the Law of *Cause and Effect* covers *all* manifestations. . . . All life in the Universe is conditioned by and responds to this law (emphasis added).[14]	When we break one of these *laws*, going against that which is *the natural order*, we have sinned . . . . *by living true to the laws that govern us we will be further blessed* . . . . breaking these laws, "sinning," will weaken and possibly destroy all that we have achieved . . . . There is a *cause and effect* relationship to sin (pp. 55–56, emphasis added).

"Be Healed!"

Healing is also sought through energy manipulation. A number of New Age therapies are based on the idea that "healing is promoted when the energy (vital life force) enveloping the body is in balance. The disease process is thought to be manifested when this energy is in a state of imbalance."[15] As long as the positive and negative aspects of the universal energy are "balanced," everything is fine.

Sickness results when the energy flow gets disrupted, imbalanced or obstructed. Balancing, or realigning, these energies within the body brings health. New Agers familiar with such terminology would immediately identify with Eadie's references to positive and negative energies. Consider the following:

> In Polarity Therapy, energy is either positive (+), negative (−), or neutral (0). . . . When energy is balanced between positive (+) and negative (−) poles . . . the "neutral" principal is manifested.[16]

Eadie never asserts that energies need to be realigned. Instead, she counsels people to attract positive energies and shun negative energies through words and thoughts. This, too, is taught by many New Agers:

New Age Movement	Embraced By The Light
"I am healthy," "I will succeed" . . . are all examples of *positive affirmations*. . . . The purpose of affirmations in metaphysical philosophy is to keep the mind and spirit focused . . . thereby drawing its beneficial effects into the physical world. The opposite would be to *dwell on the negative manifesting* in one's life . . . *since in the metaphysical world, like attracts like* (emphasis added).[17]	*Positive attracts positive, and negative attracts negative*. . . . by thinking positive thoughts and speaking positive words *we attract positive energy* (pp. 57–58, emphasis added).

Like most New Agers, Eadie feels that because our thoughts can affect this eternal energy, "they [our thoughts] are the source of creation."[18]

New Age Movement	Embraced By The Light
[W]e each create our own version of the world, our particular reality . . . (emphasis added).[19]	We create our own sur-roundings by the thoughts we think (p. 58, emphasis added).
[N]ew energies give far greater impact and *power to an individual's thinking* and feeling. . . . In the hands of a person or a group that was disor-ganized or *negative* in thought and feeling, these energies would intensify the projection of much chaos and negation . . . (emphasis added).[20]	If we understood the *power of our thoughts*, we would guard them more closely. If we understood the awesome power of our words, we would prefer silence to almost anything *negative* (p. 58, emphasis added).
[T]he *imagination* of man may produce *healthy or morbid* effects (emphasis added).[21]	Gifted people are able to use their *imaginations* to create new things; both *wonderful and terrible* (pp. 58–59, emphasis added).
The greatest *power* in heaven and earth is *thought* (emphasis added).[22]	There is a literal *power* in the creations of the mind. . . . Our *thoughts* have *tremendous power* (pp. 59, 71, emphasis added).

(continued on next page)

New Age Movement	Embraced By The Light
[T]he creative *power of the universe is within us* . . . . we must remember that *we are babies* in the new world. . . . We are now *learning to live in accordance with the true laws* of the universe (emphasis added).[23]	We are like *babies* crawling around, trying to *learn how to use the forces within us.* They are powerful *forces and are governed by laws* . . . (p. 71, emphasis added).
When pure Soul energy, evoked by the *sound* of the *words and phrases* . . . is attracted by synchronous *vibration* into contact with the thoughtform, it is *immediately* activated (emphasis added).[24]	The very *words* themselves—the *vibrations* in the air—attract one type of energy or another. . . . spiritually it is *instantaneous* (p. 58, emphasis added).

"Our thoughts," according to Eadie, "have exceptional power to draw on the negative or positive energies around us"[25] which in turn create realities. This being the case, it only makes sense to believe that a significant number of our limitations are self-imposed by "wrong thinking," especially disease.

In other words, we actually create our illnesses (as well as our healing) with the mind. By gaining control over our thoughts and learning how to properly verbalize *positive* images, we can obtain anything—even healing. New Age literature promoting these concepts is voluminous. *Embraced By The Light* is just another book on the ever-growing list:

New Age Movement	Embraced By The Light
Disease and suffering arise from a mind that is unwhole, that is filled with *confusion and despair* (emphasis added).[26]	*[M]any of the illnesses* of my life were the result of *depression or feelings* of not being loved (p. 64, emphasis added).
A *positive, life-affirming attitude* is a key in the *healing process* (emphasis added).[27]	[P]ositive self-talk begins the *healing process* (p. 65, emphasis added).
The body is just a particular form of the universal life energy, whereas *the mind* is a more subtle form, which has a greater capacity for universal attunement and harmony. Thus the *body needs to adapt itself to the mind* (emphasis added).[28]	[T]he spirit and *the mind* have tremendous influence on the flesh. . . . we literally have power to affect our own health. . . . The spirit has power to control the mind, and *the mind controls the body* (p. 62, emphasis added).
[A]ll genuine healing addresses the problem of unblocking *negativities* . . . (emphasis added).[29]	I saw that I had often yielded to *negative "self-talk"*. . . . not only did I claim these *negativisms* by calling them mine, but I opened the door and accepted them as mine (p. 64, emphasis added).

These last quotations from *Embraced By The Light* are reflective of Mind Science groups (like Christian Science) and New Thought groups (such as Unity School of Christianity), which hold that all sickness is a product of the mind. The main difference between the Mind Sciences and New Thought revolves around the *nature* of illness. The

Mind Science believers say that everything is just an illusion, whereas New Thought proponents do recognize the existence of matter.

It seems that Eadie leans toward New Thought, given her belief that we are not to deny the presence of illness.[30] Consequently, it is with New Thought that her doctrines should be compared.

According to Ralph Waldo Trine, "one of the most brilliant articulators and authors of New Thought metaphysics,"[31] healing must be performed *"by the operation of life forces within"* (emphasis added).[32] He also theorizes: "The time will come when the work of the physician will not be to treat and attempt to heal the body, but to heal *the mind, which in turn will heal the body"*. . . *(emphasis added)*.[33]

Eadie, too, contends that all healing "takes place from *within*" (emphasis added)[34] and maintains the classic New Thought belief that it is ultimately the mind which heals the body:

> [T]he spirit and *the mind* have tremendous influence on the flesh. . . . we literally have power to affect our own health. . . . The spirit has power to control the mind, and *the mind controls the body* (emphasis added).[35]

Eadie even gives instructions on how to get our minds to heal our bodies:

> Positive attracts positive, and negative attracts negative. . . . by thinking positive thoughts and speaking positive words we attract positive energy . . . . Some people use negative energy to create harmful things. . . . Others use their imaginations in positive ways. . . . Our thoughts have exceptional power to draw on the negative or positive energies around us. When they draw at length on the negative, the result can be a weakening of the body's defenses. This is especially true when our negative thoughts are centered on ourselves. . . . Once we have identified the illness or problem, we need to start verbalizing its

remedy. We need to remove thoughts of the illness from our minds and begin concentrating on its cure. Then we need to verbalize this cure, letting our words add to the power of our thoughts.[36]

These procedures for putting to use the powers of the mind are undeniably similar to New Thought technique:

> According to New Thought, human beings can experience health, success, and abundant life by using their thoughts to define the condition of their lives. New Thought proponents subscribe to the "law of attraction." This law says that just as like attracts like, so our thoughts can attract the things they want or expect. Negative thoughts are believed to attract dismal circumstances; positive thoughts attract more desirable circumstances. Our thoughts can be either creative or destructive. New Thought sets out to teach people how to use their thoughts creatively.[37]

A Biblical Perspective

Jesus never said: "Beware of the Pharisees who teach that there are positive and negative energies as well as thought power." In fact, Scripture nowhere addresses such issues specifically. How, then, do we determine if the ideas are biblical? First, we must look at where such beliefs come from and determine whether or not their doctrinal roots are unscriptural. Second, we need to find biblical passages which may indirectly relate to the particular issues being examined.

Mind Science and New Thought ideas are based on a broader set of teachings which directly contradict every essential belief of Christianity. Individuals within metaphysical groups believe: 1) the Bible is just one of many holy books; 2) everything is part of a unified whole (monism); 3) God is all and all is God (pantheism); 4) Jesus Christ was not the unique Son of God; 5) Jesus Christ did not die for our sins; 6) salvation does not come by grace through faith in Christ, but it comes through correct understanding of reality; 7) man is a divine idea, part of the Divine Mind.[38]

The particular concepts Eadie has taken from New Thought and the Mind Sciences spring from some very anti-Christian teachings. Even though she may want to isolate certain ideas, such as those encompassing negative and positive thoughts, it cannot logically be done because every New Thought/Mind Science teaching is inseparably intertwined. Only when working together with their companion doctrines do the metaphysical beliefs about "mind power" make any degree of sense. Such beliefs must therefore be rejected.

Moreover, attributing to men's minds the power to literally create reality flies in the face of numerous biblical verses which point to God as the Creator (Genesis 1:1; Isaiah 42:5). Because God is the Creator, it is to Him that we must bring our desires (Psalm 5:2, 6:9, 55:1; Philippians 4:6). Scripture never instructs us to create what we want with our thoughts and words.

There is obviously a place for positive thinking, watching our words, and doing the best we can to accomplish a task. Philippians 4:8, for example, lists numerous things upon which we should consistently dwell. Colossians 3:8, 4:6 and Titus 2:8 give instructions regarding our speech. Nowhere, however, does the Bible tell us to rely on the *power* of words or thoughts. All good gifts do not originate in our minds. They come from God. "Every good and perfect gift is from above, coming down from the Father of the heavenly lights, who does not change like shifting shadows" (James 1:17).

Even tragedies, including sicknesses, come ultimately from God rather than from our minds (Psalm 119:71, 75). Sometimes illness and/or suffering comes to us *directly* from the Lord for the purpose of chastisement (2 Corinthians 12:7; Hebrews 12:5–6). On other occasions, as in Job's case, suffering comes *indirectly* from God. Job was a righteous man before God (Job 1:1, 8, 22, 2:10), and yet God *allowed* him to be afflicted (1:12; 2:6). In other words, while Satan may have *directly* afflicted Job, it was God who *indirectly* sent the calamity (42:11). In short, God is sovereign—not our minds, not our thoughts, and not our words (1 Chronicles 29:11–12; Psalm 47:6–8, 103:19; 1 Timothy 6:15–16).

Regarding the existence of a universal "energy," this concept, too, comes from and continues to function within a very unbiblical framework. New Age expert Elliot Miller observes:

> In the New Age movement today bioenergy theory operates within the context of pantheism: all reality is God, God is impersonal but conscious energy; therefore, all reality is a manifestation of spiritual energy. And if this energy can be released man will be both healed and mystically enlightened to his true divinity.[39]

Miller is simply saying that belief in a universal energy (or energies) goes hand in hand with pantheism. This is apparent in the writings of numerous New Age personalities.

John Thie, developer of Touch for Health therapy, writes: "[The modern] chiropractor believes that the innate intelligence that runs the body is connected to universal [cosmic] intelligence that runs the world [i.e., 'God'], so each person is plugged into the universal intelligence."[40]

D.D. Palmer, a chiropractic authority, identifies the "innate" (or universal energy) in crystal clear terms:

> Innate is said to be part of the "All Wise, Almighty, Universal Intelligence, the Great Spirit, the Greek's Theos, the Christian's God, the Hebrew's Helohim [sic], the Mahometan's Allah, [homeopathy founder] Hahnemann's Vital Force, new thot's [sic] Divine Spark."[41]

Christians must reject belief in this universal energy because it is an overflow of impersonal pantheism, which, as we have already seen, is opposed to what the personal God of the universe has revealed through His Word.

There is another reason for us to not accept as true the kind of energies endorsed in *Embraced By The Light*. According to such works as the *Dictionary of Mysticism and the Occult* and the *Encyclopedia of Occultism & Parapsychology*, Eadie's positive and negative energies play important roles in the world of the occult. This is not surprising since Eadie is a practicing occultist, as the following chapter will show.

ENDNOTES

[1] Eadie, Betty. *Embraced By The Light*, p. 51.

[2] Sneed, Dr. David and Dr. Sharon Sneed. *The Hidden Agenda*, p. 239.

[3] Melton, J. Gordon, Jerome Clark and Aidan A. Kelly. *New Age Almanac*, p. 304.

[4] Weldon, John and Clifford Wilson. *Psychic Forces and Occult Shock*, p. 247.

[5] Ibid., p. 249.

[6] Vivekananda. *The Yogas and Other Works*, pp. 592–593, 598 as quoted in *Psychic Forces and Occult Shock* by John Weldon and Clifford Wilson, pp. 249–250.

[7] Kastner, Mark and Hugh Burroughs. *Alternative Healing*, p. 5.

[8] De Castro, Erwin, B.J. Oropeza and Ron Rhodes. *Christian Research Journal*, "Enter the Dragon?," Fall 1993, p. 34.

[9] Ankerberg, John and John Weldon. *Can You Trust Your Doctor*, p. 111.

[10] Eadie, op. cit., p. 57.

[11] Kastner and Burroughs, op. cit., p. 108.

[12] Eadie, op. cit., p. 57.

[13] Spangler, David. *Revelation: The Birth of A New Age*, pp. 67, 68, 71.

[14] Two Disciples. *The Rainbow Bridge*, pp. 39–40.

[15] Kastner and Burroughs, op. cit., p. 248.

[16] Ibid., p. 191.

[17] Ingenito, Marcia Gervase. *National New Age Yellow Pages*, 1987 edition, p. 151.

[18] Eadie, op. cit., p. 58.

[19] Gawain, Shakti. *Living in the Light*, p. 26.

[20] Spangler, op. cit., p. 97.

[21] Shepard, Leslie A., ed. *Encyclopedia of Occultism & Parapsychology*, vol. 1, p. 98.

[22] Dowling, Levi H. *The Aquarian Gospel of Jesus the Christ*, 84:22, p. 126.

[23] Gawain, op. cit., pp. 3, 5.

[24] Two Disciples, op. cit., p. 153.

[25] Eadie, op. cit., p. 63.

[26] Carlson, Richard and Benjamin Shield, eds. *Healers on Healing*, p. 165.

[27] Ibid., p. 147.

[28] Ibid., "Healing, Love, and Empowerment," by Jack Schwartz, p. 21.

[29] Ibid., "Healing Attitudes," by Sun Bear, p. 150.

[30] Eadie, op. cit., p. 65.

[31] McConnell, D.R. *Another Gospel*, p. 41.

[32] Trine, Ralph Waldo. *In Tune with the Infinite*, p. 43 as quoted in *A Different Gospel* by D.R. McConnell, p. 156.

[33] Ibid., p. 65 as quoted in *A Different Gospel* by D.R. McConnell, p. 156.

[34] Eadie, op. cit., p. 63.

[35] Ibid., p. 62.

[36] Ibid., pp. 57–59, 63, 65.

[37] Rhodes, Ron. *The Counterfeit Christ of the New Age Movement*, p. 149.

[38] Adapted from *Speaking the Truth in Love to the Mind Sciences* by Rev. Todd Ehrenborg.

[39] Miller, Elliot. *Christian Research Journal*, "The Christian, Energetic Medicine, 'New Age Paranoia,' " Winter 1992, p. 26.

[40] Ankerberg, John and John Weldon. *New Age Health Practices*, p. 207.

[41] Ibid., p. 212.

"THE MOST PROFOUND AND COMPLETE NEAR-DEATH EXPERIENCE EVER"

EMBRACED BY THE LIGHT

Partial Reproduction

The original cover of *Embraced By The Light* clearly portrays Eadie's "being of light" as Jesus. When the book went national, Jesus was replaced by a non-descript white light—an image which could be interpreted as anyone or anything by the non-Mormon public.

> I learned that spirits can choose to enter their mother's body at any stage of her pregnancy. Once there, they immediately begin experiencing mortality. Abortion, I was told, is contrary to that which is natural. The spirit coming into the body feels a sense of rejection and sorrow. It knows that the body was to be his, whether it was conceived out of wedlock or was handicapped or was only strong enough to live a few hours. But the spirit also feels compassion for its mother, knowing that she made a decision based on the knowledge she had.

Partial Reproduction

Top: Page 95 of a nationally-distributed version of *Embraced By The Light*. Eadie's strong stand against abortion is notably altered to be more acceptable to the general public (see Appendix A).

> I learned that spirits can choose to enter their mother's body at any stage of her pregnancy. Once there, they immediately begin experiencing mortality. Abortion, I was told, is an act against that child. The spirit feels an immediate and devastating rejection. He knows that the body was to be his, whether it was conceived out of wedlock or was handicapped or was only strong enough to live a few hours; but now it has been taken from him. What happens to that spirit, or how it is healed, I don't know.

Partial Reproduction

Bottom: Page 95 of an early edition of *Embraced By The Light*. In this Utah-issued copy, Eadie speaks out strongly against abortion (see Appendix A).

This difficult-to-obtain flyer entitled "Of Special Interest to Members of the Church of Jesus Christ of Latter-day Saints" was inserted into the first several thousand copies of *Embraced By The Light*, which were released in the predominantly Mormon "Intermountain West" region. It tells of Eadie's conversion to the Mormon Church, her desire to convert others to the LDS faith, and her status as an active Temple Mormon who once served as Ward Young Women's president. The flyer was removed from books distributed to the general public.

Saturday 1:00 pm

MICHAEL TIERRA O.M.D
The Herbal Tarot
Author of **The Spirit of Herbs** and the **Natural Remedy Bible**, Tierra is a licensed acupuncturist and herbal practitioner. Together with Candace Cantin, they will develop an intuitive model for self-healing based on The Herbal Tarot. You will learn how it is designed and methods for its use as a tool for healing.
Room 1

TIMOTHY LEARY PH.D.
How To Operate Your Brain
For over three decades, Leary has been designing and popularizing methods which empower individuals to think for themselves. After outlining the various functions of the brain and the latest technology in multi-media electronics, he will create an environment conducive to producing self-induced trance states which can help reprogram the mind.
Room 4

SANLEY McDANIELS / DANIEL DRASIN
The Martian Ruins: Spiritual Implications
Drasin is a writer and award winning media producer. McDaniels is a former Chairman of Philosophy at Sonoma State. In this illustrated discussion, overwhelming evidence will reveal that the face on Mars and other Martian structures are artificial. Discover the implications of these findings and the controversial loss of the NASA Mars Observer.
Room 7

JEANNE ROSE
Aromatherapy: Scents And Ritual
A leading pioneer in the uses of natural remedies and aromatherapy, Rose is considered the Grande Dame of American herbalism. Learn to use oils in a ritualistic sense to empower your life. This session explores the myriad aspects of aromatherapy using essential oils to trigger memories and to inspire and expand your inner strength.
Room 2

SIMONE
Inside The Healing Circle
Simone has been working as a spiritual catalyst since 1984. She will reveal methods, including meditation, guided imagery, and the healing energy of color and sound to heal the body and reacquaint yourself with your higher consciousness. Prepare yourself for a shamanic journey that will connect you with guides and animal allies in the non-ordinary worlds.
Room 6

FEATURED WORKSHOP

BETTY EADIE
Embraced By The Light
At the age of 31, Eadie died as a result of complications from surgery. Her death experience is one of the most amazing stories ever told. Compelled to share her encounter, she will recount in vivid detail what she saw and learned from the other side, what happens when we die, and the wonderful opportunities we have while we are in our physical bodies.
Room 11

Leading the Charge: Orrin Hatch and 20 Years of America, by Lee Roderick. Aspen/Gold Leaf Press. $23.00.

The Burning Within, by RaNelle Wallace with Curtis Taylor. Aspen/Gold Leaf Press, $16.95.

Page 32 of the *1994 Spring Whole Life Expo Program Guide* advertising Eadie's featured workshop. Also speaking at the New Age event were astrologers, witches, shamans, channelers, energetic medicine proponents and fellow hypnotherapists.

Page 3 and 5 of a recent issue of *IMPRESSIONS*—a Mormon magazine designed to inform Latter-day Saints of new LDS works—include advertisements by Gold Leaf Press, clearly identified as part of Aspen Books, a well-known Mormon-owned and operated publishing house. Such a link signals to LDS readers that the books are produced by fellow Mormons. In nationally circulated advertisements for the same title, however, the Aspen Books link is removed (see Appendix B).

A self-portrait by Swiss-born medium Hélèna Smith with her "guardian angel." Smith experienced astral travel and practiced automatic writing (an occult practice whereby a disembodied spirit allegedly writes through the individual they are possessing).

A leaf photographed using the Kirlian method. Occultists believe that the surrounding aura is a manifestation of the universal life force. Scientists have shown that the glow is actually due to the moisture content of objects.

A medieval painting by Hieronymus Bosch entitled "The Ascent into the Empyrean," shows a spirit enroute to heaven through a common NDE element— the long dark tunnel ending in a bright light.

ASPEN BOOKS

6211 South 380 West
Salt Lake City, Utah 84107
(801) 265-9393
FAX (801) 268-0992
Orders only: 1-800 748-4850

ORDER FORM
June 1994

Date:

BILL TO:		SHIP TO:	
ADDRESS:		ADDRESS:	
CITY:		CITY:	
STATE/ZIP		STATE/ZIP	
PHONE		NAME:	
PO#:		SHIP VIA:	

SPECIAL CLOSEOUT BARGAINS
50% DISCOUNT NON-RETURNABLE

____3018 Greg and Kellie, (1-56236-301-8),Thayers, ... $6.95 $3.95

____3050 In the Mind's Eye, (1-56236-305-0), Donla Thayer, $9.95 $4.95

____2062 Liberating Form: Mormon Essays on Religion and Literature, (1-56236-206-2), Marden J. Clark, ... $9.95 $4.95

____301 Pioneer Children Sang, Coloring Songbook, ... $1.98 $.99

____3042 Salvador, (1-56236-304-2), Margaret Young, ... $9.95 $4.95

____6151 Teaching Children the Love of Missionary Work, (1-56236-151-1), Olson\Garrison, ... $7.95 $.99

____6001 Vol. 1, Prepare to Serve, (1-56236-001-9), bk ..... $5.95 $.99

____6002 Vol. 2, Called to Serve, (1-56236-002-7), bk ..... $5.95 $.99

____6003 Vol. 3, Continue to Serve, (1-56236-003-5), bk ... $5.95 $.99

BOOKS

____3026 Abide the Dark Dawn, (1-56236-302-6), Susan Evans McCloud, ... $6.95

____3058 Burning Within, The, (1-88272-305-8), (Gold Leaf Press), RaNelle Wallace with Curtis Taylor, ... $16.95

____2046 Christmas for the World: A Gift to the Children, (1-56236-204-6), Various Authors, ... $12.95

____2054 Eliza and Her Sisters, (1-56236-205-4), Maureen Ursenbach Beecher, ... $8.95

____902 Embraced by the Light, (Gold Leaf Press), (1-882723-00-7), HB, Eadie\Taylor, ... $16.95

____3066 The Homeless Hibernating Bear, (1-88272-306-6), (Gold Leaf Press) Kids Livin' Life, ...·.......... $7.95

TO COMMEMORATE 27 JUNE 1844
THE MARTYRDOM REMEMBERED
A 150 YEAR PERSPECTIVE
ON THE ASSASSINATION OF JOSEPH SMITH
by DAVIS BITTON

____5554 I'm in the Spotlight, (0-9628216-1-6), (Dream Tree Press), Euretig, ... $11.95

____4006 Joseph Smith: A PhotoBiography, The Young Latter-day Saint's Library, Vol 1, (1-56236-400-6), HB, Susan Evans McCloud, ... $12.95

____6201 LDS Speaker's Sourcebook, The, (1-56236-201-1), Aspen Books $14.95

____315 Leading the Charge: Orrin Hatch and 20 Years of America, (1-88272-309-0), (Gold Leaf Press), HB, Lee Roderick ... $23.00

____3090 Martyrdom Remembered: A 150 Year Perspective on the Assassination of Joseph Smith, HB, (1-88272-213-5), Davis Bitton, ... $16.95

____2127 My Best for the Kingdom: History and Autobiography of John Lowe Butler, A Mormon Frontiersman, HB, (1-56236-212-7), William G. Hartley, ... $24.95

____2089 Offenders for a Word: How Anti-Mormons Play Word Games to Attack Latter-day Saints, (with F.A.R.M.S.), (1-56236-208-9), Peterson\Ricks, ... $9.95

____2070 Portrait of a Prophet's Wife: Emma Hale Smith, (Silver Leaf Press), HB, (1-56236-207-0), HB, Norma Fischer, ... $12.95

____5553 Rainbow Writing, (0-9628216-0-8), (Dream Tree Press), Euretig\Kreisberg, ... $11.95

____2100 Riches of Eternity, (1-56236-210-0), HB, ed. by John K. Challis and John G. Scott, ... $14.95

____2119 Sarah McDonald: "Bishop of the First Ward", (1-56236-2119), HB, Peggy Petersen Barton and Drew Barton Quinn, ... $10.95

____901 Successful Returned Missionary, The, 2nd Edition (Belmont Press), Bruce L. Olsen $9.95

____2003 Why I Believe, (1-56236-200-3), HB, Jake Garn, ... $11.95

____3069 Women I Have Known & Been, (1-56236-306-9), HB, Carol $11.95

TAPES

____7064 Aunt Patty Remembers/Only When 1 Laugh, (1-56236-706-4), Elouise Bell, double audio cassette $7.98

____7080 Freedom & Free Agency, (1-56236-708-0), Jake Garn, .. $6.98

____903 Embraced By The Light, Audio Book, (Simon & Schuster) Betty J. Eadie, complete book on tape, 3 cassettes, ... $19.95

____913 Embraced By The Light, The Musical Journey, tape, (1-882723-07-4), Bryce Neubert and Stan Zenk, ... $9.95

____914 Embraced By The Light, The Musical Journey, CD, (1-882723-08-2), Bryce Neubert and Stan Zenk, ... $14.95

____7048 Mormonism and the Arab World, (1-56236-704-8), Dr. Daniel Peterson $5.98

____7951 My Everlasting Friend, (1-56236-795-1), tape, Bryce Neubert $9.95

____7943 My Everlasting Friend, (1-56236-794-3), CD, Bryce Neubert, ... $14.95

____7072 My Journey Beyond, Pt 1, (...-702-1), Betty Eadie, . $7.98

____7099 My Journey Beyond, Pt ?, ...t Eadie, . $7.98

____7056 A Secret Something?, ... -56236-705-6) ... ongs for b...

YOUNG WOMAN VALUE WREATH

____401 Card (Single) $1.50

____402 Card (Package of 6) $5.95

____403 Bookmark .... $.99

____406 Bookmark w/values printed on it .... $.99

____404 Print, medium, (8 X 10) $5.95

____405 Print, large, (9 X 12) $6.95

____407 Matted Print, small $6.95

____408 Matted Print, medium $8.95

____409 Matted Print, large $10.95

____410 Framed Print, order desired color $28.00

WASATCH REVIEW INTERNATIONAL

"Wasatch Review International" is a M... ...iannual literary journal containing short stories, personal essays, poetry ... ...ews.

____801 Volume $6.00

This June 1994 ordering form from the Mormon-owned and operated Aspen Books of Murray, Utah (which owns Gold Leaf Press) includes such titles as *The LDS Speaker's Sourcebook* and *Offenders for a Word: How Anti-Mormons Play Word Games to Attack Latter-day Saints*.

Dr. Raymond Moody

Dr. Elisabeth Kübler-Ross

Dr. Michael Sabom

Dr. Kenneth Ring

Dr. Melvin Morse

Dr. Bruce Greyson

Page 955 from a 1991 metro-
Seattle telephone book listing
Eadie's advertisement for her
hypnotherapy practice.

Betty Eadie, author of *Embraced By The Light*

CHAPTER 8

The Dark Side of the Light

Of the Bibles that are sent to me with requests to write a short message on the flyleaf, more come from Mormons than from any others.

— Jeanne Dixon, astrologer[1]

Behind all of its 20th century packaging, pseudo-scientific terminology, and socio-political agendas, the New Age movement is little more than occultism. *Time* magazine has called the New Age "a combination of spirituality and superstition, fad and farce, about which the only thing certain is that it is not new."[2]

Every technique New Agers use to gain spiritual "truth" can be traced either directly or indirectly back to the ancient mystery religions of Egypt, Babylon, Chaldea and other pagan cultures. The movement provides a perfect illustration of Ecclesiastes 1:9–10:

What has been will be again,
   what has been done will be done again;
   there is nothing new under the sun.
Is there anything of which one can say,
   "Look! This is something new"?
It was here already, long ago;
   it was here before our time.

The word *occult* (derived from the Latin *occultus*) basically means "hidden/secret" things. The term encompasses a broad range of practices including astrology, numerology, witchcraft, crystal gazing, necromancy (communication with the dead), magic, palm-reading, tarot cards, channeling, automatic writing, seances, ouija boards and dowsing. All of these satanically energized methods of obtaining otherwise unobtainable knowledge are forbidden to man and cursed by God (Exodus 22:18; Leviticus 20:6; Acts 19:19).

Occult practices are the primary means through which New Age teachings are proclaimed. Despite their modern-sounding names (e.g., astral projection, psychometry, radiance therapy), they are the same practices that Christians have been standing against for more than 19 centuries.

One such activity—hypnosis—is especially relevant to us because Betty Eadie is a hypnotherapist.[3] A hypnotherapist is a registered counselor who uses hypnosis to help people modify unwanted feelings or behaviors (e.g., smoking, over-eating, stress, fear, etc.).[4] Eadie's occultic profession has been briefly mentioned in only a few newspaper articles. Rarely, if ever, has it been made known that Eadie had her own hypnotherapy practice until very recently (perhaps as late as 3/13/93).[5]

The media has also never discussed at length Eadie's other occultic beliefs and practices. But now that *Embraced By The Light* is influencing Christians, Eadie's occult connection can no longer be ignored.

The Hypnotic Eye

Hypnosis is a practice whereby an individual is placed into an altered state of consciousness known as a "trance." No one really knows the true nature of this trance,[6] but it is most often termed an "artificially induced kind of sleep state."[7] It has further been described as an "altered awareness, although the conscious mind is still present."[8]

The *New Age Almanac* explains that this artificially induced sleep state is characterized by "increased suggestibility in the subject" (p. 57). In fact, most subjects are *very* susceptible to the suggestions that they are given while hypnotized.[9] One's capacity to accept suggestions is "the key to hypnotism's ability to effectively accomplish its goals."[10]

The function of hypnotherapy is to "recondition certain sensory reactions to the stimuli of anxiety or psychic [mental] tension so that instead of producing physiological symptoms, such as ulcers or headaches, they fail to do so."[11]

Hypnotherapists "relax their subjects progressively, often by using a countdown numbering procedure or by progressively relaxing the body limb by limb from the feet to the head."[12] Once the client has been fully hypnotized, the therapist is then able to address that individual and make suggestions which will affect his or her actions and/or feelings after being awakened. If necessary, the patient can even speak to his or her therapist while hypnotized. The subject can also be made to either remember or forget what transpired during the session.

Thousands of medical physicians, registered counselors and psychiatrists maintain that hypnosis has successfully treated "blindness, paralysis, inability to speak or sing, personality disorders, alcoholism, addiction to nicotine, obesity, sexual problems, phobias such as fear of heights, water, flying in airplanes, driving over bridges, enclosed spaces and many others. . . . In the field of medicine it is used in anesthesiology, obstetrics, surgery, psychiatry. . . . In dentistry it can be used to alleviate anxiety and reduce pain and discomfort."[13]

Numerous health care professionals feel that hypnosis is the greatest discovery since penicillin. And it must be admitted that many hypnotherapists have good intentions and admirable goals. Unfortunately, hypnosis is a doorway to the demonic which, once opened, is difficult to close.

Those well-acquainted with hypnotism acknowledge that its long history is "inextricably interwoven with occultism . . . ."[14] In *An ABC of Witchcraft Past and Present*, celebrated witch Doreen Valiente writes: "There is no doubt that, under many different names, hypnosis has been known from very early times and practised as a secret technique of magic."[15] Valiente also describes in her book the various ways that witches have for centuries used hypnosis to accomplish a number of tasks.

New Age authors Mark Kastner and Hugh Burroughs agree

131

that hypnosis is very old. Their investigation reveals that hypnotic-like behavior "has been reported from the dawn of history. Hypnotherapy in the form of waking and sleeping suggestion is among the oldest of the healing arts."[16] Like Valiente, Kastner and Burroughs see hypnosis as something deeply embedded in occult history:

> In ancient Egypt, priests used hypnotic incense and chanting to induce a state sometimes known as "temple sleep" during which curative suggestions were given. . . . During the Golden Age of Greece, the Abatons had "sleep temples of the sick." People would be put into prolonged sleep induced by soft music, repeated phrases, and drugs. Shamans, medicine men, and witch doctors used drums, objects of fixation, music, costumes, and ritual dance to induce trance states during which they would make waking suggestions of healing.[17]

Hypnotism's close link with occultism may explain several disturbing byproducts of the therapy which consistently emerge in the lives of hypnotic subjects. These include inner revelations of unbiblical doctrines, a heightened interest in the occult, contact with the dead (solicited and unsolicited) and demonic possession.

The most common false doctrine associated with hypnosis is reincarnation—an Eastern religious belief which asserts that every person has either lived, or will live, numerous lives on earth. Each lifetime is supposedly necessary in order to reach perfection (i.e., evolve to the point of assimilation back into the oneness of an impersonal pantheistic god).

Reincarnation and hypnotism began to be associated with one another after past lives unexpectedly started "popping up" during hypnotic sessions. It happened so often that a form of hypnosis called hypnotic regression was designed specifically to regress people to their childhood, past their birth, and back into previous lives.

Such a use for hypnotism, commonly called "Past Lives Therapy,"[18] was initiated by the many hypnotherapists who adopted the idea that one's problems in *this* life may be the result of unresolved issues in a *previous* life. The answer seemed almost too simple: go back and resolve those past-life problems through hypnosis. They do not seem to have considered Hebrews 9:27, which tells us that men are appointed to [live and] die only once.

In fairness to Eadie, it should be noted that she does not believe in reincarnation.[19] A rejection of that doctrine, however, does not mean that the practice of hypnosis is acceptable. Hypnotism persistently gives rise to erroneous teachings.

There is another problem with hypnosis: it tends to increase one's desire to participate in the occult. According to a variety of sources, hypnotism can be a very quick pathway to increased psychic phenomena and heightened spiritual awareness. Clairvoyance, a supernatural ability to receive information through visual images that appear in the mind, is often another result of hypnosis. Many occultists, in fact, use hypnotic trances to gain greater psychic abilities. This reason alone is enough to put hypnotism in a category marked "off-limits" for Christians.

Two more aspects of hypnosis must be mentioned: contact with the dead and demonic possession. These, however, are not really byproducts of the practice, but are instead alternate goals that hypnotists and their subjects sometimes pursue. In such cases, the "sleep state" is more properly referred to as a mediumistic trance, or a trance induced by a medium, which is an "intermediary for communication between the material and spirit world."[20]

According to The Steinerbooks Dictionary of the Psychic, Mystic, Occult, the mediumistic trance "is a sleep-like condition which enables the subject's body to be used by a discarnate [bodyless] spirit."[21] That there exists a connection between spirit possession and hypnosis is common knowledge. Take, for example, the following statement from the Encyclopedia of Occultism and Parapsychology: "The mediumistic trance is recognized as having an affinity with hypnosis . . . ."[22]

In the same volume, under the heading "Hypnotism and Spiritualism," it is suggested that contact with the dead (necromancy) through hypnosis is rooted in witchcraft and modern spiritism:

Witchcraft, in which the force of hypnotic suggestion seems to have operated in a very large degree, was thought to result from the witches' traffic with the devil and his legions. Even in some cases the souls of deceased men and women were identified with these intelligences, although not generally until the time of Swedenborg [an 18th century spiritist].[23]

Despite its evil origins, hypnosis has indeed been used to correct many physical as well as psychological problems. When evaluating such merits, however, Christians must bear in mind that the practice is closely connected with false doctrines and full-blown spiritism. Both are explicitly condemned by God. "Do not eat any meat with the blood still in it" (Leviticus 19:26). (Leviticus 19:31; Deuteronomy 18:9–12; Jeremiah 27:9; Ezekiel 13:9). Hypnotism, because it encourages evil behavior (i.e., occultism), also falls under the condemnation of First Thessalonians 5:22, which tells us to abstain from every form of evil.

Eadie's Auras

On page 58 of *Embraced By The Light* Eadie writes: "I saw different energies surround different people. I saw how a person's words actually affect the energy field around him."

This section of Eadie's book reflects her belief in the occult concept of "auras." On page 79, she uses this very term when describing a heavenly garden where the plant's surfaces were difficult to define because "of each plant's intense aura of light."

In occult literature, the aura is virtually synonymous with the universal energy force (i.e., prana, chi, ki, etc.) permeating all that is.[24] A precise definition of the aura appears in the *Encyclopedia of Occultism and Parapsychology*:

An emanation said to surround human beings, chiefly encircling the head, and supposed to proceed from the nervous system. It is described as a cloud of light diffused with various colors.[25]

Eadie shares this occultic view of auras. Note the similarity between her words and those found in *An Encyclopedia of Psychic Science*:

Occultism	Embraced By The Light
Clairvoyants often claim the ability to see the human *aura*. From its colours they draw inferences as to the *emotional state* or character (emphasis added).[26]	Our *auras*, or countenances, display the *feelings* and *emotions* of our souls (p. 91, emphasis added).

Auras are said to indicate everything from a person's health to his or her emotional state. But not everyone can see auras. According to the *Dictionary of Mysticism and the Occult*, these multi-colored indicators of our physical, mental and emotional condition can only be observed by psychics:

> **Aura.** In occult terminology, the psychic energy field that surrounds both animate and inanimate bodies. The aura can be dull or brightly colored, and psychics—those who claim to perceive the auric colors directly—interpret the quality of the person or object according to the energy vibrations.[27]

A psychic (or clairvoyant) is a person who allegedly possesses "paranormal powers or extrasensory perception: precognition, clairvoyance, mental telepathy, ability to see and diagnose the aura."[28] Sometimes psychics are called "sensitives," especially when referring to their ability to sense information or see auras. This particular description of psychics is the one Eadie seems to favor.

The following compares Eadie's views with those expressed in the *Encyclopedia of Occultism and Parapsychology*. The excerpt from the occult volume is discussing occultist Baron von Reichenbach and his "odic force," a precursor to auras:

Encyclopedia	Embraced By The Light
Reichenbach claimed to have discovered a new force . . . which could be seen in the form of flames by "sensitives," i.e., *sensitive individuals* or psychics (emphasis added).[29]	God sees them [auras] . . . . Even very *sensitive people* here can see them (p. 91, emphasis added).

In an attempt to prove the existence of auras, occultists habitually point to a photographic technique known as Kirlian photography, which is supposedly able to capture on film the auras of animate as well as inanimate objects. This process was accidentally discovered in 1958 by Soviet electrician Semyon Kirlian. The *Dictionary of Mysticism and the Occult* explains what happened:

> While repairing an instrument in a research institute, he noticed an unusual effect occurring with a subject undergoing electrotherapy. Tiny flashes of light passed between the electrodes and the person's skin, and Kirlian thought he would try to photograph the discharge. . . . Kirlian succeeded in photographing a luminous "corona" around his fingers. . . . Kirlian believes that his corona-photographs reveal energy levels in living objects. . . . subsequent Kirlian researchers have compared the vivid colors in Kirlian photographs with the color variations in the **aura** allegedly perceived by psychics.[30]

Only occult sources appeal to Kirlian photography as "proof" of a universal energy. In scientific literature, "the phenomenon has long been sufficiently explained in terms of the moisture content of animate and inanimate objects—without reference to any vital energy."[31]

Acceptance of auras is basically an endorsement of occult phenomena. It is also an affirmation of psychics because they are supposedly the only ones able to "read" auras.

Moreover, auras are linked to belief in a universal energy—again, Eadie is supporting doctrines and practices which stand in direct opposition to God's Word.

Unholy Visitations

There is another compelling reason to reject Eadie's teachings. She has numerous spirit guides who, ever since her near-death experience, have periodically visited her. In *Embraced By The Light*, Eadie refers to these guides as "guardian angels" that she met while "dead" (pp. 32, 90). These "angels" were even mentioned by her on "The Oprah Winfrey Show":

> There were three spiritual beings that appeared in my room and they explained to me that they were my guardian angels. And as they talked to me I knew that I knew them.[32]

It is not necessarily wrong or unbiblical to believe in guardian angels. Matthew 18:10 is commonly appealed to by many Christians as a proof text for guardian angels. As Billy Graham writes:

> Some believe strongly that each Christian may have his own guardian angel assigned to watch over him or her. This guardianship possibly begins in infancy, for Jesus said, "See that you do not look down on one of these little ones. For I tell you that their angels in heaven always see the face of my Father in heaven" (Matthew 18:10).[33]

Some Christians, however, feel that passages such as Matthew 18:10 refer to angels "who are charged with the care of believers as a group (Hebrews 1:14)," and that there is not sufficient warrant for the idea "that each individual believer has a particular angel assigned to him."[34]

Others shy away from believing in guardian angels because the concept of individually assigned spiritual protectors has much to do with occultism. In occult literature, guardian angels are identified as spiritual beings who are in charge of protecting a medium either while in a trance or when functioning normally. These entities, also known as "doorkeepers,"[35] are believed to be personal, protective spirits that overview "one's day-to-day activities and provide warnings of impending danger."[36]

The well-known occultist Edgar Cayce, who often entered sleep-like trances to receive communications from the spirit world, taught that guardian angels are actually a part of our own spiritual selves. The function of the "guardian angel" is to keep us attuned to the energies of the One. His views were recently discussed in *Venture Inward*, a magazine published by the Association for Research and Enlightenment, the organization he founded in 1931:

> [C]ayce sees a portion of our being as the angel, the guardian angel. He describes the guardian angel as "The companion of each soul as it enters into a material experience. [It] is ever an influence for the keeping of that attunement between the creative energies or forces of the soul-entity *and* health, life, light, and immortality."[37]

Occultists often refer to guardian angels as "guiding spirits" from whom information is received. The *Encyclopedia of Psychic Science* explains:

> **Guiding spirits**, or guardian angels . . . escape experimental verification. According to seance room communications everyone has guiding spirits. . . . Torquato Tasso, according to Hoole's *Life of Tasso*, ended his career by believing that he had a familiar spirit with whom he conversed, and from whom he learnt things which he had never read or heard of, and that indeed were unknown to other persons (p. 154).

These types of messengers have often appeared to Eadie since her 1973 near-death experience. In recounting one such visitation she writes: "That night I was awakened by a messenger who stood by my bed. I understood that he had come from the spirit world. He said that the situation with my baby was not right, that she would be returned to me."[38]

When I spoke with Eadie in January of 1994, I asked if she continues to receive visits from her spirit world "friends." She responded without hesitation: "Yes, I have." Eadie went on to confirm to me that she may one day even write a book chronicling the visits.

In the January 9, 1982, issue of the *Psychic News*, a very interesting question appeared:

> Do you believe, as many Spiritualists do, that you have a spirit guide who has been watching over you for many years, perhaps since your birth, and will be waiting to welcome you on your arrival in the next world?[39]

Embraced By The Light gives us Eadie's answer:

> "I'm dead," I thought. . . . three men suddenly appeared at my side. . . . they, with others, had been my guardian angels during my life on earth.[40]

Eadie says she is "not comfortable with spirit guides."[41] At the same time, however, she continues to welcome her guardian angels "wholeheartedly" whenever they present themselves to her.[42] During a WMUZ radio interview, she reconciled this apparent contradiction when she said, "I want to receive all of my information directly from Him [God] and not through any spiritual guides *unless* He [God] sends it that way."[43] In other words, Eadie does not proactively seek out spirit guides, but when such guides present themselves as having been sent from God, she welcomes them.

Whether or not angels could be appearing to Eadie is not the issue here. Scripture tells us that angels do exist (Psalm 148:2; Hebrews 1:5). As the great reformer John Calvin wrote:

> The angels are the dispensers and administrators of the divine benificence toward us; they regard our safety, undertake our defense, direct our ways, and exercise a constant solicitude that no evil befall us.[44]

139

The Bible also affirms that angels can indeed appear to people (Luke 1:19; 26) and that there has been a fall of angels (Matthew 25:41; 2 Peter 2:4; Jude 6). The chief result of this fall being demons (Matthew 8:16; Luke 10:17–18; Acts 19:12–16; Revelation 16:14) or spiritual forces of wickedness (Ephesians 6:12).

The important question is: How do we know what kind of angels (guides), if any, have appeared to Eadie? One need only look at the doctrines these entities have presented. As we have seen in previous chapters, the "truths" Eadie has learned through her "guardian angels" are unbiblical. Consequently, we can only assume that her eternal "friends"—if they truly exist—are demonic (holy angels do not preach unholy doctrines).

Only this conclusion makes sense when one also considers Eadie's other occultic beliefs and practices. God, as well as His people, do not have fellowship with the unfruitful works of darkness (2 Corinthians. 6:14–15; Ephesians 5:11).

Something to Think About

A 1977 Roper poll reportedly indicated that 114 million Americans were either directly or indirectly involved in the occult.[45] A variety of statistics that have since emerged show that millions of Americans continue to have a relationship with occultism:

- At least 42 percent of American adults believe that they have "been in contact with someone who has died."[46]
- Approximately 67 percent of American adults claim to have had a psychic experience such as extrasensory perception (ESP).[47]
- One out of every three American adults believe that fortunetellers can foresee the future.[48]
- Forty-three percent of all teens believe in ESP.[49]
- Seventy percent of baby boomers believe in psychic powers.[50]
- A 1993 poll showed 14 percent of the American public agreed that "horoscopes and astrology usually provide an accurate prediction of the future."[51]

• A growing list of Hollywood occultists includes: Shirley MacLaine, a multi-talented actress, believes in channeling, reincarnation and psychic abilities; Linda Evans, star of "Dynasty," is a close friend of and believer in famous channeler J.Z. Knight; LeVar Burton of "Star Trek: The Next Generation," firmly believes in crystal power; Marina Sirtis, also of "Star Trek: The Next Generation," practices tarot card reading.

What kind of people are being drawn toward Eadie's occultic beliefs? Christian writer W. Elwyn Davies, in *Principalities and Powers*, identifies the various types of individuals who consistently seem to be interested in occult phenomena:[52]

• The curious, who experiment with demonic forces without having a fully formed system of religious beliefs. A number of teenagers, for example, get involved in the occult due to nothing more than curiosity.
• The conformist, who looks around at his or her peers and says, "Everyone does it," and then decides "to be another who 'does it'."
• The dissatisfied, "whose religious experience has left him unfulfilled and skeptical."
• The sad, "whose bereavement inclines him towards anything that offers knowledge of the dead."
• The rebellious, "who recoils from the status quo in the church and in society, and seeks a viable alternative elsewhere."
• The psychically inclined, "who wants to develop suspected latent powers."
• The children of practicing occultists, "who are conditioned from childhood."
• The credulous, who are ready to believe just about anything and everything.

It is fairly obvious that Eadie has plenty of company in the world of the occult. She is also not alone in claiming to have died and come back to life. A 1991 Gallup Poll survey found that "12 percent of American adults report that they have survived a near-death experience (NDE)."[53] This percentage, when applied to a 1991 population estimate of 252,160,000,[54] means that some 30,259,200 people have allegedly "died" and come back to life. Of those who have actually reported their NDE, nearly all have returned from the spirit world espousing doctrines remarkably similar to those being taught by Eadie.

There is a clear connection here between the success of *Embraced By The Light* and the public's familiarity with occultism and NDEs. Consequently, our examination of Eadie's book would not be complete without a brief examination of NDEs and those individuals who have placed them in the forefront of American thought.

ENDNOTES

[1] Dixon, Jeanne. *My Life and Prophecies*, p. 208.

[2] *TIME*, 12/7/87, "New Age Harmonies," p. 62.

[3] n.a. *U.S. West Direct Yellow Pages*, 1991 edition, p. 955; cf. Miller, Leslie. *USA Today*, "Betty Eadie, Shedding 'Light' on Her Visit to Heaven," 8/12/93, p. 5D.

[4] n.a. *U.S. West Direct Yellow Pages*, 1991 edition, p. 955.

[5] Price, Kathie. *The Arizona Republic*, "Visiting Death: Woman Tells of Glimpse of Paradise," 3/13/93, p. B7.

[6] Fodor, Nandor. *Encyclopedia of Psychic Science*, p. 388.

[7] Rudolf Steiner Publications. *The Steinerbooks Dictionary of the Psychic, Mystic, Occult*, p. 101.

[8] Kastner, Mark and Hugh Burroughs. *Alternative Healing*, p. 124.

[9] Ibid., p. 126.

[10] Ibid.

[11] Lande, Nathaniel. *Mindstyles/Lifestyles*, p. 87.

[12] Drury, Nevill. *Dictionary of Mysticism and the Occult*, p. 258.

[13] Kastner and Burroughs, op. cit., p. 126.

[14] Shepard, Leslie, ed. *Encyclopedia of Occultism and Parapsychology*, vol. 2, p. 642.

[15] Valiente, Doreen. *An ABC of Witchcraft Past and Present*, p. 224.

[16] Kastner and Burroughs, op. cit., p. 124.

[17] Ibid., pp. 124–125.

[18] Ibid., pp. 183–184.

[19] Eadie, Betty. *Embraced By The Light*, p. 93.

[20] Fodor, Nandor. *Encyclopedia of Psychic Science*, p. 232.

[21] Rudolf Steiner Publications, op. cit., p. 218.

[22] Shepard, op. cit. vol. 3, p. 1370.

[23] Ibid., vol. 2, p. 649.

[24] Kastner and Burroughs, op. cit., p. 194.

[25] Shepard, vol. 1, op. cit., p. 97.

[26] Fodor, op. cit., p. 17.

[27] Drury, Nevill. *Dictionary of Mysticism and the Occult*, p. 21.

[28] Ibid., p. 216.

[29] Shepard, op. cit., vol. 2, p. 647.

[30] Drury, op. cit., p. 143.

[31] Miller, Elliot. *Christian Research Journal*, "The Christian, Energetic Medicine, 'New Age Paranoia,' " Winter 1992, p. 27.

[32] Eadie, Betty. "The Oprah Winfrey Show," 1/3/94 (reaired 8/3/94).

[33] Graham, Billy. *Angels: God's Secret Agents*, p. 98.

[34] Pfeiffer, Charles F. and Everett K. Harrison, eds. *The Wycliffe Bible Commentary*, p. 962.

[35] Rudolf Steiner Publications, op. cit., p. 90.

[36] Drury, op. cit., p. 106

[37] Van Auken, John. *Venture Inward*, "Guides, Angels, and Holy One," July/Aug. 1994, pp. 16–17.

[38] Eadie, *Embraced*, op. cit., pp. 139–140.

[39] Masters, Martin. *Psychic News*, "Are All Met on Entering the Beyond?," p. 7.

[40] Eadie, *Embraced*, op. cit., pp. 30, 32.

[41] Eadie, Betty. WMUZ interview with Al Kresta, 3/3/94.

[42] Ibid.

[43] Ibid.

[44] Calvin, John. As quoted in *Angels: God's Secret Agents* by Bill Graham, p. (iii).

[45] Weldon, John and Clifford Wilson. *Psychic Forces and Occult Shock*, p. 104.

[46] Chandler, Russell. *Understanding the New Age*, p. 20.

[47] Ibid.

[48] Morin, Richard. *The Sacramento Bee*, "A Revival of Faith in Religion," 7/4/93, p. 1.

[49] n.a. *Religion Watch*, "Current Research: Recent Findings on Religious Attitudes and Behavior," 2/93, p. 3.

[50] Roof, Wade Clark. *The Denver Post*, "The Four Spiritual Styles of Baby Boomers," 3/21/93, p. 4.

[51] Barna, George. *The Barna Report 1992–93*, p. 258.

[52] Adapted from *Principalities and Powers* by W. Elwyn Davies as quoted in *Handbook of Today's Religions*, p. 153.

[53] Lueders, Beth. *Clarity*, "Out of Body or Out of Your Mind," May/June 1994, p. 28.

[54] U.S. Department of Commerce. *Statistical Abstract of the United States 1993*, 113 ed., p. 8.

PART 3

AN
EXPERIENCE
CALLED
DEATH

I sort of floated into this tunnel and there were other figures that I recognized. And this welcoming sun, white sun, and warmth, and like being in liquid mercury. It was like being weightless. . . . It was in all the papers that I had died.

— Elizabeth Taylor, actress[1]

CHAPTER 9

Learning How to Die

*Come sweet death! be persuaded O beautiful death! In
mercy come quickly.*

— Walt Whitman, American author[2]

Only once during my childhood did I get a glimpse of the
Grim Reaper. His everpresent spectre briefly material-
ized when my maternal grandmother died. But because I
was just a small boy, the quiet conversations, hushed sobs,
endless hugs, and most of all, the seriousness of the whole
situation, barely intruded upon the fringe of my consciousness.

One event at the funeral home, however, lodged vividly in
my young mind. I was a rather rambunctious child, and had
unfortunately decided to let out some youthful energy by
chasing my older brother in the presence of several
mourners. With my tie undone and size five suit jacket in
hand, I rounded a particularly sharp corner only to find my
mother there to greet me. Even if I had not seen her, the
sudden, viselike grip around my arm coupled with a complete inability to continue my pursuit would have immediately alerted me to her presence.

"You boys stop this running around right now," she scolded. "You just don't understand." Her last words broke with the kind of raspy quality only grief can produce. Tears began to fill her eyes, and she walked away.

For the rest of that day I was as good as gold. I was also puzzled. Mom's words kept coming back to me: "You just don't understand." She was right. But nobody seemed willing, or able, to alleviate my ignorance. No one wanted to talk. I learned then and there that death was something to be experienced rather than discussed.

As a teenager I still did not know much about dying. In fact, I hardly ever thought about it. Death, after all, was not an especially relevant topic for me and my friends. Consequently, I had no way of knowing how to react when I was told that "Grandpa," (my paternal grandfather) had died. A thousand different responses shot through my mind in the span of maybe one-thousandth of a second. In the end, I chose to do that which had worked best during my last encounter with death—say nothing. I never even told my father how sorry I was that his dad had died. I simply did not know how to say such things.

A year after graduating from high school a phone call in the middle of the night informed me that three former classmates had been killed in an automobile accident. An icy freeway had claimed their lives as they were traveling home for Christmas vacation from a southern Illinois university. It was time for me to come to grips with the one thing in life that everyone must eventually face—death.

I had difficulty responding to death because I grew up during an era when it was still a taboo subject. As recently as 1977, three years before my friends died, an article in *Human Behavior* magazine read: "[O]ur educational system teaches us precious little about how to live and nothing at all about how to die or cope with another's death."[3] My generation had no classes about relating to a terminally ill friend. Nor were there courses on what to say to those in mourning. And there were certainly no popularized methods for coping with one's own grief.

Things are different today. Countless books cover the subject of death. Everything from how to emotionally handle the loss of a loved one to ways of facing one's own imminent death have been examined and dealt with from nearly all angles. The number of such books continues to increase, especially now that the AIDS epidemic is taking so many lives.

This openness about death started back in 1969 when Swiss-born psychiatrist Elisabeth Kübler-Ross became persuaded through her work with terminally ill patients in Chicago that the whole subject of death "should be confronted and discussed much more openly."[4] She herself had faced the temporality of life as a nurse to World War II refugees and to Polish survivors of the Nazi Holocaust.

In order to accomplish her monumental task in America, the determined psychiatrist not only asked the question "How do we die?" but also "possessed the simple genius to ask it of the only people who could really answer—people who were themselves dying."[5] Her findings were published in *On Death and Dying*, the first bestseller of its kind.

Queen of Death

For two and half years prior to the publication of *On Death and Dying*, Kübler-Ross worked with hundreds of terminally ill patients who taught her about "the final stages of life with all its anxieties, fears, and hopes."[6] Her book retold these stories so others would be encouraged to not shy away from those facing death. Its basic message was simple: get closer to those dying because much can be done for them in their final hours.[7]

Kübler-Ross also promised that people taking her advice would receive a mutually gratifying experience and learn "much about the functioning of the human mind, the unique human aspects of our existence, and will emerge from the experience enriched and perhaps with fewer anxieties about their own finality."[8]

Thousands found comfort through *On Death and Dying*. It received rave reviews from such notable publications as the *American Journal of Psychiatry* and the *Journal of the American Medical Association*.[9] Kübler-Ross was almost instantly catapulted to "world renown as a pioneering authority on the psychological aspects of death . . . ."[10] She was even named a *Ladies' Home Journal* "Woman of the

Decade" for the 1970s.

Part of what made *On Death and Dying* so popular was how it divided the dying process of terminally ill patients into the now-famous five stages of grieving: denial, anger, bargaining, depression and acceptance. The final stage was a state of peace and tranquillity. "Watching a peaceful death of a human being," she writes, "reminds us of a falling star; one of the million lights in a vast sky that flares up for a brief moment only to disappear into the endless night forever."[11]

Kübler-Ross learned that death, rather than being a curse to fear, was actually a blessing to be welcomed. Her redefining of death gave birth to what would come to be known as the "death awareness movement"[12] or "the death and dying movement."[13] Home care for the terminally ill, hospices, the heated topic of euthanasia, the debate over one's right to die with dignity and a host of other death-related issues all owe their existence to Kübler-Ross.

A New Perspective

Kübler-Ross had never considered herself a religious person, but she began to change after noticing two common occurrences among dying patients: 1) on their deathbeds they "often spoke to people—apparently to someone who had preceded them in death"; and 2) after the moment of clinical death, "most of them got a look of incredible peace on their faces."[14]

Kübler-Ross' research took a radical turn when several of her patients told her that they had "traveled in spiritual form" while clinically dead for various lengths of time.[15] One woman patient by the name of Mrs. Schwartz told Kübler-Ross how, while lying unconscious from internal bleeding, she "regained awareness and found herself floating above her body. She could see everything in the room—the doctors, the nurses, their attempts to resuscitate her—but she could not speak to them. Mrs. Schwartz said she reentered her body as it was being wheeled to the morgue, and she startled the attendants by pulling the sheet away from her head."[16] Subsequent investigations of similar stories finally convinced Kübler-Ross of "a higher reality of the spirit."[17]

In her search for more answers about life after death, the once skeptical doctor started dabbling in the occult via self-induced out-of-body experiences (astral projection), a practice that allegedly enables a person's soul/spirit to voluntarily leave the body and travel to other spiritual dimensions, or higher realms of consciousness (i.e., the spirit world).

Kübler-Ross' first out-of-body experience (OBE) occurred accidentally in approximately 1974 at the end of an extended workshop, which left her exhausted. "I had several dying patients who needed my absolute, full presence and alertness for a whole week," she recounted.[18] When she finally fell asleep at around 5 a.m. during the last night of the workshop, "she suddenly felt herself separate from her body as 'a whole bunch of beings' began to work on it."[19]

After a two-hour nap, Kübler-Ross returned to her body rested and refreshed. A woman companion who had been in the room while Kübler-Ross slept reported that the unconscious Kübler-Ross had actually appeared as though dead—having no pulse or respiration. This same companion concluded that an out-of-body experience had taken place.[20]

Kübler-Ross wasted no time in reading up on OBEs and subsequently contacted Robert A. Monroe, a Virginia businessman who in the 1970s turned his studies of OBEs and other occult-related issues into a full-time occupation.[21] Kübler-Ross soon visited the investigator of the paranormal at his Monroe Institute for Applied Sciences in rural Virginia. Her hopes were to learn how to voluntarily initiate OBEs through meditation techniques.

"[W]hen I had my first experiment," recounts Kübler-Ross, "I went too fast, and he [Monroe] interfered when I was just at the ceiling. He called me and I went 'kerplunk' back into my body. I was mad as could be. It was the first time I was able to do it on command, and it was a big thrill that it actually worked."[22]

The next time Kübler-Ross induced an OBE, she made sure that Monroe would not impede her:

[T]he moment we started, I said to myself, "I am going so fast that nobody has ever gone that fast, and

I am going further than anybody has ever gone." And at that moment when I said that, I took off faster than the speed of light. I felt like I must have gone a million miles. . . . The moment I was going at the speed of light horizontally, I switched and made a right-angle turn, rounded a big hill and went up. . . . It is incredible to get to a place where there is no time and space."[23]

Deeper into the Dark

After mastering the ability to produce an OBE at will, Kübler-Ross continued seeking information about life and death through occultic, rather than scientific methods. The more she made use of metaphysical practices, the more her scientifically-minded colleagues questioned her credibility. She drew especially harsh comments from them by publicly declaring in 1974 that she believed in life after death "beyond a shadow of a doubt."[24]

But she continued undaunted in her explorations of the mystical. Kübler-Ross had grown accustomed to being criticized, noting in one interview that in 1968 she was being "spat at in the hallways of hospitals for helping dying patients."[25]

At some point during her many disembodied journeys into the spirit world, Kübler-Ross allegedly made contact with numerous "spirit guides" and started counseling the living "to make their decisions based on the guidance of entities from the Other Side."[26] Her main guide was reportedly Salem, "a handsome Egyptian-looking man with a brownish face and hairy arms."[27] She would eventually have three more spirit entities serving her: Mario, Anka and Willie.[28]

Serious doubts about Kübler-Ross' mental stability began circulating when, at a September of 1976 gathering of more than 2,300 people, she claimed that "through the concentrated effort and combined energy of seventy-five people singing together somewhere in California" she witnessed the physical materialization of these spiritual beings with whom she regularly conversed.[29]

According to an article that appeared in the November/December 1976 issue of *Yoga Journal*, Kübler-Ross said:

Last night I was visited by Salem, my spirit guide, and two of his companions, Anka and Willie. They were with us until three o'clock in the morning. We talked, laughed and sang together. They spoke and touched me with the most incredible love and tenderness imaginable. This was the highlight of my life.[30]

As the 2,000 plus attendees sat stunned by the above admission, Kübler-Ross unloaded another bit of news that unsettled her listeners:

She then played a tape recording of a male friend of hers playing the guitar and singing "You Are My Sunshine" and "I'll Be Loving You Always," accompanied by a second male voice that she said was one of her guides.[31]

Whether or not Kübler-Ross really witnessed the physical manifestation of spiritual entities is debatable. Barring the possibility that her whole story is contrived, Mark Albrecht and Brooks Alexander of Spiritual Counterfeits Project make two observations about Kübler-Ross' 1976 experience:

The first is that what is described here can only be classified as a form of concourse with the forbidden spiritual realm (necromancy) and therefore bears the full weight of the relevant biblical warnings and judgments [Ex. 7, 8, 22:18; Lev. 19:26, 31, 20:6, 27; Deut. 18:9–12; Is. 8:19]. The second point is that the *quality* of the manifestations Dr. Kübler-Ross speaks of are characteristic of a deep and prolonged involvement with spiritistic practices. Sustained, external, public displays by spirit beings do not normally occur unless there has been a considerable belief-commitment and surrender of will to the spirit(s) involved.[32]

Many in the scientific community began looking upon the once respected Dr. Kübler-Ross as someone who had somehow been "bewitched into buying every last spiritualist trick in the book."[33]

Through hypnotic regression, for example, she claimed to

153

have reexperienced her own birth.[34] Kübler-Ross then claimed to have gone back even further than birth, recalling a past life she had lived during the time of Jesus. The doctrine of reincarnation, she maintained, had been "taught in Christianity for hundreds of years" until it was purged from the church for political reasons.[35] People cannot "return to God with dirty hands," she warns. "You have to come back and make good for all your mistakes."[36]

She also came to believe that all biblical references to eternal conscious punishment (hell) only symbolized the sorrows we will feel when during an after-death life review, we realize how many times we have failed to show love.[37]

> [Hell is] self-imposed and self-inflicted as we are forced to evaluate our lives and realize where in our whole existence we took "lower choices rather than higher choices," particularly where we chose to act unlovingly rather than lovingly. . . . we learn lessons about ourselves by being made totally aware of whatever pain or suffering any of our actions have ever caused another human being. "It is incredibly logical. . . . no man could invent such a fair system."[38]

The Final Straw . . . Almost

Kübler-Ross' reputation took its most serious blow in 1980 when a sex scandal broke out in the Church of the Facet of Divinity, a religious sect linked to Shanti Nilaya, the organization Kübler-Ross created to help dying patients deal with their imminent deaths. She had joined forces with the church's psychic healer/medium leader, Jay Barham, in the late 1970s. Barham had been touted by Kübler-Ross as "the greatest healer in the world."[39]

Former members of Barham's church felt differently. The following is only one of many accounts which exposed what was really going on in the spiritist church:

> Barham regularly conducted seances in which he acted as a medium to communicate with what he called "afterlife entities." At many of these sessions,

the former female members of the group asserted, they were instructed to enter a side room where they were joined a few minutes later in the dark by an unclothed man who talked convincingly of being an 'afterlife entity' [who] . . . then proceeded to convince the women that they should engage in sex with him[40] . . . .

Barham's antics might never have been discovered had it not been for an overly curious female devotee who flipped on the lights during one of her spiritual trysts. Instead of seeing the physical manifestation of a guide from "the other side," she saw Barham—wearing nothing but a turban.[41]

A year later Kübler-Ross was still defending and working with Barham. Finally, however, the negative publicity had become too great and she condemned him as a fraud. Why did she work with him for so long after he was exposed? Kübler-Ross said she was doing her own "first-person investigation" of him.[42] Few accepted her defense.

Despite the scandal, Kübler-Ross' work did not end. Neither did her popularity. By 1982 she had received 20 honorary degrees and had taught an estimated "125,000 death-and-dying courses in colleges, seminaries, medical schools, hospitals, and social-work institutions."[43]

Kübler-Ross (now based in Head Waters, Virginia) is still active in NDE research. As of 1993, she had collected "more than 20,000 stories from people of all ages and cultures who claim to have seen the light."[44] Although she has not written a book since 1987, she continues to teach hundreds of death and dying workshops every year.

Theologically, she might best be described as a New Ager. In fact, she wrote a brief essay on healing that was included in the 1989 New Age book *Healers On Healing*, which featured such New Age luminaries as Shakti Gawain, Ram Dass, Bernie Siegal and Deepak Chopra.

"The healer," she writes, "must act as a channel—that is, as the conduit of a healing entity or force, whether one calls this God, Christ, the Inner Teacher, or whatever."[45]

Kübler-Ross' involvement with the occult is now fairly well-known. What is not widely known is the fact that her occult experiences actually began prior to the publication of

On Death and Dying. Shortly before the book's release, she was visited by an apparition identifying itself as none other than Mrs. Schwartz, the patient who had confirmd to Kübler-Ross that life existed beyond the grave.

Mrs. Schwartz reportedly appeared to Kübler-Ross soon after dying in order to "thank Elisabeth for having taken care of her and to encourage her to continue her work with dying patients . . . ."[46] Part of that continuing work was the gathering of information about patients who had clinically died and returned to tell about what they had experienced.

Kübler-Ross was even going to write a book specifically addressing the subject, but a fellow-psychiatrist by the name of Raymond A. Moody beat her to it when in 1975 he published *Life After Life.* It quickly became a classic (as of 1994 it had sold 12 million copies).[47]

The foreword to *Life After Life* was written by Kübler-Ross. A more qualified person could not have been chosen to give the book a much-needed vote of support. She was, after all, the recognized "Queen of Death."[48] Within a few short years, however, Moody would be the King.

ENDNOTES

[1] Taylor, Elizabeth. "The Oprah Winfrey Show," 3/4/93.

[2] Whitman, Walt. "The Wound-Dresser" as found in *English Poetry in Three Volumes: From Tennyson to Whitman,* vol. 3, edited by Chalres W. Eliot, p. 1409.

[3] Nietzke, Ann. *Human Behavior,* 1977, "The Miracle of Kübler-Ross" as reprinted in *Cosmopolitan,* 2/80, p. 206.

[4] Constable, George, ed. *Psychic Voyages,* Mysteries of the Unknown Series, p. 64.

[5] Nietzke, op. cit.

[6] Kübler-Ross, Elisabeth. *On Death and Dying,* preface.

[7] Ibid.

[8] Ibid.

[9] Ibid., back cover.

[10] Nietzke, op. cit.

[11] Santmire, Paul H. *The Christian Century*, 12/14/83, "Nothing More Beautiful Than Death," p. 1157.

[12] Rosenbaum, Ron. *Harper's*, 7/82, "Turn On, Tune In, Drop Dead," p. 32.

[13] Santmire, op. cit.

[14] Nietzke, op. cit., p. 208.

[15] n.a. *The Mother Earth News*, "The Plowboy Interview: Elisabeth Kübler-Ross On Living, Dying . . . and Beyond," p. 17.

[16] Constable, op. cit., p. 65.

[17] Ibid.

[18] Nietzke, op. cit, p. 209.

[19] Ibid.

[20] Ibid.

[21] Ibid.

[22] Ibid.

[23] Ibid.

[24] Constable, op. cit., p. 64.

[25] n.a. *The Mother Earth News*, op. cit., p. 22.

[26] Rosenbaum, op. cit., p. 40.

[27] Nietzke, op. cit., p. 211.

[28] Rosenbaum, op. cit., p. 41.

[29] Nietzke, op. cit.

[30] Kronisch, Lennie. *Yoga Journal*, "Elisabeth Kübler-Ross: Messenger of Love," p. 20 as quoted in *Journal of the Spiritual Counterfeits Project*, "Thanatology: Death and Dying," April 1977, by Mark Albrecht and Brooks Alexander, p. 8.

[31] Nietzke, op. cit.

[32] Albrecht, Mark and Brooks Alexander. *Journal of Spiritual Counterfeits Project*, "Thanatology: Death and Dying," April 1977, p. 8.

[33] Rosenbaum, op. cit.

[34] Nietzke, op. cit., p. 210.

[35] n.a. *The Mother Earth News*, op. cit., p. 21–22.

[36] Ibid., p. 21.

[37] Ibid., p. 22.

[38] Nietzke, op. cit., p. 208.

[39] Rosenbaum, op. cit.

[40] Ibid., p. 42.

[41] Ibid.

[42] Ibid.

[43] Ibid., p. 32.

[44] Haas, Jane. *Orange County Register*, "Into the Light," 1/10/93, p. 1 (Accent Section).

[45] Carlson, Richard and Benjamin Shield, eds. *Healers on Healing*, "The Four Pillars of Healing" by Elisabeth Kübler-Ross, p. 127.

[46] Nietzke, op. cit., p. 211.

[47] Summer, Bob. *Publisher's Weekly*, "Near-Death Success," 8/16/93, p. 31.

[48] Rosenbaum, op. cit.

CHAPTER 10

Long Live the King

It is research such as Dr. Moody presents . . . that will enlighten many and will confirm what we have been taught for two thousand years—that there is life after death. . . . I think we have reached an era of transition in our society. We have to have the courage to open new doors and admit that our present-day scientific tools are inadequate for many of these new investigations.

— Elisabeth Kübler-Ross[1]

Psychiatrist Raymond A. Moody was introduced to near-death experiences while still a philosophy student at the University of Virginia in the mid-1960s. There, he heard a professor of psychiatry—George Ritchie—describe how, as a soldier during World War II, he had died for nine minutes during an especially serious bout with influenza.[2] "In some unimaginable way," Ritchie recounted, "I had lost my firmness of flesh, the body that other people saw."[3]

Like the familiar near-death experiences of today, Ritchie hovered over his body in spirit form, passed through walls and moved from place to place at lightning speeds. He chose to return to his body so he could fulfill a lifelong desire to attend medical school. Upon reentering the hospital room where his lifeless body still lay, a most extraordinary thing allegedly happened:

Suddenly, the room was filled with an intense illumination, and Ritchie saw that a man made of light had appeared. From inside himself he heard the words, "You are in the presence of the Son of God." Simultaneously, his whole life, "every event and thought and conversation, as palpable as a series of pictures," he said later, passed before him in review. Then Private Ritchie woke up in his own body . . . . [4]

Moody was unable to forget Ritchie's story. His curiosity was further piqued a few years later when, while teaching in North Carolina, a student told him another life-after-death account.[5] By the time Moody entered medical school in 1972, he had already begun collecting similar reports from all over the country. Out of the 150 cases that ended up on his desk, only a handful (perhaps 50) were included in *Life After Life*.

Moody's bestseller also included the first use of the term "near-death experience" (NDE) as well as a never-before-seen list of the 15 elements that recur among NDEs.[6] He further established that the exact number of elements contained in a particular NDE depends upon how long a person remains "dead." According to Moody, the chronology of the elements varied as well. He additionally found that no NDE had *all* 15 elements, but that every NDE had at least one of the following:[7]

- **Ineffability.** People who have experienced an NDE say they cannot adequately express what happened to them. In their attempts to decribe the NDE, many have remarked: "There are just no words to express what I am trying to say," or "They just don't make adjectives and superlatives to describe this." (*Life After Life*, p. 26).

- **Hearing the News.** Several persons have reported hearing their doctors or other onlookers pronounce them dead (p. 26).

- **Feelings of Peace and Quiet.** Many describe extremely pleasant feelings or sensations during the beginning stages of their experiences even though severe pain is thought of as accompanying a fatal injury or disease (p. 28).

• **The Noise**. In many cases, distinct sounds are heard either at, or near, death. Sometimes they are pleasant (e.g., Japanese wind bells, beautiful music, etc.). On other occasions, extremely harsh and disturbing sounds such as a bad buzzing noise, a loud ringing or click, a roaring, a banging or a wind-like whistling sound (pp. 29–30).

• **The Dark Tunnel**. Most people have a sensation of being pulled very rapidly through a dark space usually described as either a cave, an enclosure, a tunnel, funnel, vacuum, void, sewer, valley or cylinder (pp. 30–31).

• **Out of the Body**. Nearly all who have an NDE remember looking at their physical body from a point outside of it, as though they were a spectator or a third person in the room who was watching figures and events in a play or in a movie (pp. 34–35).

• **Meeting Others**. Several persons have recounted that at some point during their NDE they became aware of other spiritual beings who had apparently arrived to ease the NDEr through their transition into death or to tell them that their time had not yet come (p. 55). Sometimes these beings appear as loved ones who have passed away, strangers who have died or some other spirits who identify themselves as guardians.

• **The Being of Light**. The element which has "the most profound effect" on NDErs is their encounter with a very bright light. When the light first appears, it is usually quite dim (as if far away), but it gradually gets brighter until almost blinding in brilliance. Despite the light's intensity, it does not hurt the eyes or prevent the NDEr from seeing his or her surroundings (p. 58). All of Moody's initial NDE subjects identified the radiant light as a *personal* being who emanated irresistible love and warmth and communicated to them telepathically, or without words (p. 60). Since 1975, however, many NDErs have described "the light" as simply an impersonal energy force. Interestingly, this impersonal force can still emanate very *personal* expressions such as unconditional love and acceptance.

• **The Review.** Several people go through an extraordinarily rapid and panoramic review of their life, which is meant to "provoke reflection" about how they lived. It is incredibly vivid and real. The images are reportedly vibrant color, three-dimensional, moving and often accompanied by the emotions and feelings experienced that were originally felt at the time of the scene being viewed (p. 65). Some characterize this episode as "an educational effort" by the being of light. During the life review the being seems to stress the importance of two things: Learning to love other people and acquiring knowledge (p. 66). No judgmental statements of any kind are given by the being of light.

• **The Border or Limit.** In a few instances, persons describe a border or limit that prevents them from journeying any further. It has taken various forms: a body of water, a gray mist, a door, a fence or a line (p. 73).

• **Coming Back.** All of Moody's subjects obviously returned from their near-death experience. Most of them said they do not know how or why they had returned. Some felt obliged to return to complete unfinished tasks. Others were actually told to come back because it was not yet their time. The majority of Moody's subjects were not necessarily "happy" to be back, especially those who had gone far enough into their NDE to meet the being of light with whom they wanted to stay (pp. 77–84).

• **Telling Others.** Those who have had NDEs never doubt the validity of their experience (p. 84). Nevertheless, the skepticism of others often prevents them from openly sharing their story (p. 85).

• **Effects on Lives.** Few try to proselytize, or try to convince others that what they experienced really happened. Many feel their lives are "broadened and deepened" and that because of the experience they are more thoughtful and philosophical about life (p. 89). Others report that life is more precious to them. In a small number of cases, individuals had gained intuition bordering on psychic. "Lessons" learned from an NDE usually focus on the importance of "love for others." Obtaining academic and experiential "knowledge" in this life is also emphasized for those who have had an NDE (pp. 89–93).

• **New Views of Death**. Most who have had an NDE no longer feared physical death because doubts about an afterlife no longer existed for them (p. 96). Death is nothing but a transitional state to another realm of life. Fear was also alleviated for many when they discovered there was absolutely no judgment that would be imposed on them by a transcendent being (e.g., the being of light, God, etc.).

• **Corroboration**. Many persons "report being out of their bodies for extended periods and witnessing many events in the physical world during the interlude" (p. 98). For example, some individuals with no medical knowledge have been able to precisely describe the emergency procedures taken to save their lives. Others have been able to accurately repeat conversations and other incidents which occurred in other parts of the hospital while they were "dead." They apparently observed them while traveling in a disembodied state (pp. 99–100).

Science: A Veil for Religion

Moody's stated purpose for producing *Life After Life* appears quite harmless. "My hope for this book," he writes in his introduction, "is that it will draw attention to a phenomenon which is at once very widespread and very well-hidden, and, at the same time, help create a more receptive public attitude toward it."[8]

But according to religion writer Jerry Yamamoto, who produced a lengthy critique of near-death experiences for the *Christian Research Journal*, a subtle agenda does emerge from Moody's book that "inclines the unwary reader toward a particular world view."[9]

The world view to which Yamamoto refers is hinted at rather boldly by Moody on page 4 of *Life After Life*: "I believe that all the great religions of man have many truths to tell us, and I believe that no one of us has all the answers to the deep and fundamental truths with which religion deals."[10]

This is the New Age belief that all religions are equally valid. It is also the world view held by Elisabeth Kübler-Ross, who has expressed the hope that someday there will be "one universe, one humankind, one religion that unites us all in a peaceful world."[11]

Life After Life contains another Kübler-Rossism: denial of a literal heaven and hell. Moody not only denies the reality of such concepts, but he also misdefines them, caricaturizes them and relegates them to the status of mythology. By doing so, he clearly leaves his position as an objective observer and becomes a subjective commentator:

> [I]n all the reports I have gathered, not one person has painted the mythological picture of what lies hereafter. No one has described the cartoonist's heaven of pearly gates, golden streets, and winged, harp-playing angels, nor a hell of flames and demons with pitchforks. So, in most cases, the reward-punishment model of the afterlife is abandoned and disavowed, even by many who had been accustomed to thinking in those terms.[12]

J. Isamu Yamamoto responds:

> Moody describes the afterlife as a place full of love and acceptance—devoid of a supreme being who makes any judgment about people's lives or character [at least from the standpoint of eternal consequences]. . . . The "mythological" picture of an afterlife with rewards and punishment is replaced with a being of light who responds, not with righteous indignation against sin, but with understanding and even humor at our shortcomings. Thus, the character

of a supreme being that Moody presents from his observations of NDEs is quite different from the character of the infinitely just and merciful (offering complete forgiveness through faith in Jesus Christ) God portrayed in the Bible (whose heaven, by the way, is also different from Moody's cartoon portraits).[13]

Throughout the mid- to late 1970s, Moody worked very closely with Kübler-Ross, even filling in for the celebrated expert on death, if she was unable to attend a speaking engagement. Eventually, Moody's research of afterlife possibilities led him down the same path Kübler-Ross had walked. It led straight into the occult.

Seers from Antiquity

Even in *Life After Life,* Moody's leanings toward occultism can be seen through appeals made to occultic sources (i.e., *The Tibetan Book of the Dead*, an eighth century work, and the writings of Emmanuel Swedenborg [1688–1772], which he apparently feels contain striking parallels to NDEs).[14]

Since at least 1984, Moody has been seriously involved in various occultic forms of divination including crystal ball gazing.[15] Such practices have gone relatively unnoticed not only by the general public, but also by the scientific community. Only now, since the October 1993 release of his newest book entitled *Reunions: Visionary Encounters with Departed Loved Ones*, is the extent of Moody's occultic involvement beginning to come to light.

Reunions culminates eight to 10 years of research Moody has conducted on how to contact the dead through occultic methods. The beginnings of his preoccupation with getting in touch with those who have passed on before us was explained to me during a July 26, 1994, telephone interview with Lonnette Brawner, Moody's administrator.

According to Brawner, Moody noticed a "common denominator" among those who had reported having an NDE. Whenever they got to the tunnel and went into the light they saw "apparitions of their deceased loved ones standing there and communicating with them."[16]

165

Moody reportedly began to wonder: "If we have an NDE, and if we can see these deceased loved ones upon death, is there a means by which we can communicate with them in life?"[17]

To answer this question, he embarked on a search through history, mythology and various world cultures to find the most successful means of contacting the dead. After dabbling with different techniques of divination, he soon found himself being drawn toward "clear-depth gazing," also known as skrying (or scrying).[18]

Skrying is a very old form of divination in which "the practitioner gazes at a shiny or polished surface to induce a trance-state in which scenes, people, words or images appear as part of a psychic communication. The familiar crystal ball of the gypsy fortune-teller provides the best example; but mirrors, polished metal, coal or bone, and even cups of clear liquid have also been used for skrying."[19]

Brawner admits, "He [Moody] got into crystal-ball gazing for a while and things of this nature. I think what mainly prompted him to go for this particular technique is because of various things that he had read . . . ."[20]

Although Moody had become convinced that skrying was the ideal means of contacting the dead, crystal ball gazing simply did not work for him. Consequently, he began experimenting with other skrying techniques. It was among the oracles of the ancient Greeks that he discovered what would become his chosen tool for contacting departed spirits—a mirror.[21]

I found Moody's choice surprising since ancient Greek skrying—known as catoptromancy—had much more to do with simple divination (the art of foretelling the future)[22] than with necromancy, which, although considered a *form* of divination, is often more specifically thought of as contacting the dead.

Brawner cleared up my confusion. Moody's years of research had uncovered information indicating that the Grecian use of mirrors extended into necromancy:

> Different cultures have different techniques that they use. The Greek culture just happens to be one culture that he [Moody] found very intriguing and

upon doing a phenomenal amount of research actually found that there are a number of oracles of the dead in Greece, or oracles themselves in Greece, that used some form of clear depth gazing, again, for communication with the dead.[23]

After settling on both the occultic method and the specific technique for contacting the dead, Moody proceeded to establish a base of operations from which to continue his "experiments." He chose Anniston, Alabama, the site of his retirement home. There, he has established what he calls his "Theater of the Mind."

Rendezvous with the Dead

"What is this Theater of the Mind?" I asked Moody's administrator.

"The facility that he [Moody] has here [Anniston] is a research facility that he used for a short time during the research that he did for the *Reunions* book."

"But what exactly is it?"

"[The place] is fashioned after the Greek culture, what they called in Greek culture a necromanteum, which is a facility where numbers of individuals would journey from far distances to [engage in a] clear-depth gazing technique to facilitate apparitions of the deceased."[24]

Brawner went on to say that Moody's whole purpose for contacting departed souls is to further his work in grief therapy. She also explained the rationale behind this therapy:

> [Moody] has hit upon a tool that we find to be very, very important in the field of grief therapy. All of the individuals that go through this research, and that have been through this technique, have lost loved ones. They all claim after going through this process that it has been a very healing process . . . .[25]

Moody has found that in cases where a person dies either in an accident or sudden illness, survivors are left with words they never had a chance to say to the deceased. Unresolved conflicts also haunt survivors. Moody's solution is to bring the dead back from the grave.

"This is basically a tool we have found to be very formulative to allowing them that time and giving them that time with that person," says Brawner. "This alleviates a lot of the grief and a lot of anxiety that they have."

From all the historical and mythological information Moody had read, he was apparently able to devise his own modern day necromanteum, which he calls a psychomanteum. What is a necromanteum/psychomanteum?

"It's a booth set up basically to gaze. You gaze into a mirror," Brawner told me. "When you're gazing into that mirror it gives you that clear-depth facilitation ability to where you can hopefully see apparitions of the deceased."[26] Moody's claimed success rate, if true, is nothing less than phenomenal:

> A number of different personalities and individuals that have gone through this technique have claimed that they have indeed seen visions, or apparitions, of deceased loved ones in the mirror—some of which have actually had verbal communications, some of which have had physical touch, some of which have reported telepathic communication with this individual. . . . Moody's success rate has been somewhere around 40%–50%. . . . There are people that don't have anything occur at all. We've had certain individuals. . . . get back home or back to their hotel room, or whatever—two to three days later, to two weeks later—have reported having some kind of experience once they get home. . . . usually it's some type of spontaneous apparitional experience. We had one woman who actually went home—and it was about two weeks later after she had gone through the process—actually reported having a spontaneous apparition with her son in which her son actually picked her up and set her back down again. It depends on the individual.[27]

Moody has, of course, had his own apparitions:

He reports in the book *Reunions.* . . . of him actually going through the mirror gazing process and at the point that he went through nothing really occurred . . . . he actually had gone through the mirror gazing technique to see, I believe it was his maternal grandmother. When nothing occurred he . . . thought nothing of it. . . . A couple of days later he reported while sitting in the living room . . . his paternal grandmother appeared to him and they held quite a lengthy conversation and of course, this was an apparition of her.[28]

Inside the Necromanteum

In Part 2 we discussed the dangers of hypnotism and its link to the occult. Moody's practice of skrying is but an off-shoot of that trance-inducing practice. The *Encyclopedia of Occultism and Parapsychology* reveals that crystal gazing is actually a form of self-induced hypnosis which helps free one's telepathic powers.[29]

Skryers place themselves into what is termed a "hypnagogic" state by gazing into a crystal ball (or a mirror). This altered state of consciousness—similar to the condition we all experience between waking and sleeping—is what allows Moody and those who use his technique to make contact with "the other side."

The following account describes in great detail exactly what leads up to, and what takes place after, a trip into Moody's Necromanteum/Psychomanteum:

> The technique itself basically involves a full day with an individual that has pre-chosen who they would like to try to have a reunion with—a deceased love one. We ask them to bring momentos of that individual, whether it be photographs, personal articles, things of that nature. We usually get started . . . talking to the individual for a short time . . . getting them in touch with the emotional aspect of the individual that they would like to have a reunion with. . . . what the person was like, what the person looked like, what type of personality the individual

had, whta the person may have disliked about the loved one. . . . we will talk to them about the individual's death as well. . . . when that individual found out about that person's death how they felt. Was the person ill? How the person died. . . . We will take them into the psychomanteum. . . . a small room . . . with an old Victorian chair that we've actually cut the legs off of, so that the chair actually sits very low to the ground. The mirror . . . is probably about a 3 x 4 mirror [plain] . . . that we have hanging in the psychomanteum. The participant will sit down in the chair. . . . We use about a 15 watt light bulb sitting just directly behind the chair to reflect just a little bit of light. . . . We ask the person just to relax, and kind of get themselves prepared for whatever they may experience. . . . We leave them in there for about 45 minutes to an hour and let them gaze. . . . your body basically slows down to a point of "you're not asleep, but you're not awake". . . . It's called the hypnagogic state. . . . Once you reach this point, then, is usually when you're more susceptible to having something happen. . . . Once the time limit is up we go in and get the individual. . . . you go through approximately an hour or two [of venting], depending upon what the person saw. . . . once they have vented to the facilitator everything that they feel is pertinent . . . they, of course, are free to go.[30]

Moody and his subjects fail to recognize the possibility that much of what is occuring in the Theater of the Mind may be the result of self-deception. Also discounted is the possibility that malevolent entities could very easily be disguising themselves as departed "loved ones." Prior to entering the psychomanteum, participants are literally handing over everything a demonic spirit would need in order to pull off such an impersonation: photographs of the deceased; their character/personality traits; information about relationships; events surrounding the death; family member reactions.

Spiritual entities with such information could manifest themselves quite convincingly as "Uncle Harry" or

"Grandma Jones." Even an ordinary human being with a little acting experience, some professional make-up, and a trick mirror could pull off an appearance as a departed "loved one."

Exactly what is happening in Moody's contemporary necromanteum is impossible to know. The Theater of the Mind is currently closed to the general public. Only "professionals, therapists and counselors" are allowed to come and learn the skrying technique of grief therapy. Brawner told me that these professionals learn the procedure so they can integrate it into their own therapeutic facilities.[31]

"From time to time," said Brawner, "we've had therapist training weekends where we actually invite psychiatrists, psychologists, therapists, educators and other interested professionals to participate in small seminars and experiential programs that employ the altered states of consciousness and the mirror-gazing technique for purposes of education, entertainment and spiritual advancement."[32]

Moody's method of "contacting" the dead is slowly gaining popularity. His organization gave me the names of six psychological counselors located in various parts of the country from California to Georgia who are using his new form of grief therapy. According to Brawner, their numbers are increasing.

One leading NDE researcher reveals that "there is some very considerable interest on the part of a number of people now to replicate these experiences that Dr. Moody has been claiming, and that these efforts are now going forward and apparently with some success."[33]

The great prophet Isaiah, in a statement particularly relevant for today, warned:

> When men tell you to consult mediums and spiritists, who whisper and mutter, should not a people inquire of their God? Why consult the dead on behalf of the living? To the law and to the testimony! If they do not speak according to this word, they have no light of dawn. Distressed and hungry, they will roam through the land; when they are famished, they will become enraged and, looking up-

ward, will curse their king and their God. Then they will look toward the earth and see only distress and darkness and fearful gloom, and they will be thrust into utter darkness. (8:19–22)

Moody's Legacy

Moody and several of his colleagues formed the Association for the Scientific Study of Near-Death Phenomena in 1978. Their research generated a flood of articles. Stories about NDEs began appearing not only in medical literature, but also in psychological, philosophical, and religious publications.

By 1980, "a dozen books detailing near-death experiences were on the market."[34] In recent years, a series of "Light" books has appeared: *The Light Beyond, Transformed by the Light, Closer to the Light, Beyond the Light, Saved by the Light* and, of course, *Embraced By The Light.*

The new challenges and questions raised by the likes of Kübler-Ross and Moody have given rise to a whole new set of NDE researchers. This second wave of investigators are doing more research about NDEs than their predecessors ever dreamed of doing.

NDE accounts are no longer being simply collected as anecdotes. Scientific "studies" of them have been launched. NDEs are being categorized, analyzed and above all legitimized. Those now associated with near-death studies are helping to form networks of support groups for NDErs. Some of the more open-minded researchers have even gone so far as to say that there is indeed a *possibility* that life after death exists. That is a big step for scientifically-minded unbelievers.

Thanks to this new breed of spiritually tolerant psychiatrists, psychologists and physicians, the scientific community's acceptance of an existence beyond the grave has never loomed closer. Unfortunately, the spirituality being propagated by most of these NDE researchers is patently nonchristian. In some ways, a new religion is forming based on the information being obtained through NDEs. Christian author Dr. Maurice S. Rawlings calls it "the religion worshipping heaven as a benevolent gift to everyone."[35] This because a majority of NDErs believe that heaven is a place of unconditional love and acceptance that awaits all men regardless of their beliefs. Adherents to this new faith of whom Betty Eadie is a clear symbol even have their own NDE sanctuary—the International Association for Near-Death Studies (IANDS).

ENDNOTES

[1] Moody, Raymond. *Life After Life*, foreword by Elisabeth Kübler-Ross, n.p.

[2] Constable, George, ed. *Psychic Voyages*, Mysteries of the Unknown Series, pp. 56–58.

[3] Ibid., p. 57.

[4] Ibid.

[5] Ibid., p. 66.

[6] Ibid.

[7] Adapted from "The Near-Death Experience" by J. Isamu Yamamoto, *Christian Research Journal*, Spring 1992, pp. 22–23.

[8] Moody, op. cit., p. 5.

[9] Yamamoto, J. Isamu. *Christian Research Journal*, "The Near-Death Experience," Sring 1992, p. 23.

[10] Moody, op. cit., p. 4.

[11] Kübler-Ross, Elisabeth. *Death: The Final Stage of Growth*, p. 3.

[12] Moody, op. cit., p. 97.

[13] Yamamoto, op. cit., pp. 23, 30.

[14] Moody, op. cit., pp. 119–127.

[15] Brawner, Lonnette. Author's 7/26/94 interview with Brawner (Moody's administrator).

[16] Ibid.

[17] Ibid.

[18] Ibid.

[19] Drury, Nevill. *Dictionary of Mysticism and the Occult*, p. 241.

[20] Brawner, op. cit.

[21] Ibid.

[22] Shepard, Leslie A. *Encyclopedia of Occultism and Parapsychology*, vol. 1, p. 212.

[23] Brawner, op. cit.

[24] Ibid.

[25] Ibid.

[26] Ibid.

[27] Ibid.

[28] Ibid.

[29] Shepard, op. cit., vol. 1, p. 285.

[30] Brawner, op. cit.

[31] Ibid.

[32] Ibid.

[33] Ring, Kenneth. Author's 7/22/94 interview with Ring.

[34] Pearson, Mark. *Rocky Mountain News*, "Into the Light: Near-Death Experiences," 3/15/89, p. 48.

[35] Rawlings, Maurice S. *To Hell and Back*, p. 106.

CHAPTER 11

Flatliners

These near-death experiences are a matter of curiosity that get immediate attention versus pawing through Scripture. If these experiences don't fit with Scripture, they are to be rejected.

— Dr. Millard Erickson, Southwestern Baptist Seminary[1]

Moody's Association for the Scientific Study of Near-Death Phenomena was incorporated as the International Association for Near-Death Studies (IANDS) in 1980-1981 by psychologist Kenneth Ring, psychiatrist Bruce Greyson and John Audette M.S. The group's promotional literature states that it was set up to "meet the needs of early researchers and experiencers [those who have had an NDE]."[2]

As "the only organization in the world devoted to the study of near-death and similar experiences and their relationship to human consciousness,"[3] IANDS has become a virtual clearing house for information about NDEs. It also sponsors near-death research and offers support services for NDErs.[4] The organization's officially stated purpose is threefold:

1) **To provide reliable information** to caregivers, experiencers, and the public by publication of the quarterly newsletter *Vital Signs*; working with the

media around the world; sponsoring an annual North American conference and other programs; and production of a wide variety of educational material.

2) **To encourage interest in research and professional applications** through publication of the quarterly *Journal of Near-Death Studies*; management of a program of small grants to encourage scholarly research; and sponsorship of occasional research seminars.

3) **To facilitate support and networking services.**[5]

Membership in IANDS is not based upon whether or not a person has had an NDE (although a vast majority are, in fact, NDErs). Anyone can join on a paid dues basis. General membership ($45 yearly) includes a quarterly newsletter, *Vital Signs*, plus access to the group's computer network. Research membership ($80 yearly) includes an additional subscription to the group's scholarly *Journal of Near-Death Studies.*[6] A lifetime membership including all benefits is available for a one-time fee of $750.

IANDS has experienced a very respectable growth rate given the narrow subject matter upon which all of its activities are focused. As of early 1994, the Connecticut-based national organization had some 1,200 members. This figure grows to 3,000-4,000, however, if one takes into account those involved in the 30-40 local IANDS chapters scattered across the country.[7] Worldwide IANDS membership is unknown, but its branches are currently located in at least a dozen different foreign countries[8] with a membership representing "every continent but the Antarctic."[9]

The acceptance of all religions as being valid and of equal worth is a common belief of IANDS members. Any exclusivistic claims, like those found in Christianity, are considered narrow-minded and "religious." This view is coupled with another New Age doctrine—everyone gets saved (whatever "saved" may mean). Many IANDS members also hold to monism and pantheism.

Dr. Elizabeth Hillstrom, a psychology professor at Wheaton College in Illinois, has attended several IANDS conferences and reports in *Clarity* magazine that people at IANDS pretty much take the "universalistic position that you don't have to be a Christian to go to heaven."[10] An examination of what has been said and written by some of the most notable members of IANDS clearly reveals that Hillstrom is correct.

Dr. Kenneth Ring (IANDS cofounder, former president)

When it comes to near-death studies, IANDS' first president, Dr. Kenneth Ring, is surpassed in notoriety only by Kübler-Ross and Moody. Ring began looking at NDEs in 1977, the same year he became acquainted with Moody. To this day, Ring considers himself "good friends" with the recognized father of NDE studies. According to Ring, the scientific community would be "far poorer" if Moody and Kübler-Ross had not conducted their pioneering research.[11]

Ring's 1981 book *Life at Death: A Scientific Investigation of the Near-Death Experience* was the first major work on NDEs to appear after *Life After Life*. His research, however, differed considerably from Moody's. Ring not only collected NDE stories, but also analyzed them "with graphs and statistical tables"[12] in an attempt to "determine whether a single pattern could be constructed from their accounts."[13] He found that certain feelings, perceptions, and experiences were indeed shared by the people he interviewed.[14]

In 1984, he produced *Heading Toward Omega*. In this sequel to *Life At Death* he came to the startling conclusion that near-death experiences are not necessarily just near-*death* experiences. They can occur even if a person has not really died. He found that the core elements of NDEs have "*nothing inherently to do with death or with the transition into death*" [emphasis added] and that what happens to an individual during an NDE "*is not* unique to the moment of apparent imminent death."[15] According to Ring, "being in a situation where death *might* have occurred as a result of some injury or accident could precipitate very much the same kind of experience."[16]

What exactly, then, is an NDE? Ring suggests that NDEs should be considered "one of a family of related mystical experiences, similar to some Indian forms of enlightenment."[17] He has additionally proposed that "the NDE itself might just be an evolutionary mechanism for moving individuals into the next stage of human development. Perhaps . . . such occurrences unlock previously dormant spiritual potential and help to produce a higher mode of consciousness."[18]

Ring believes that there is definitely "a conscious existence after our physical death"[19] and that coming close to death is perhaps only "one avenue to a higher 'frequency domain,' or reality, which will be fully accessible to us after what we call death."[20]

Two major doctrines of the New Age movement are that all religions are equally valid, and that there is no "one way" to God. Such views, observes Ring, are what NDEs are all about:

> I don't want to imply that this is something that goes against any particular religion, it doesn't. The NDE is something that fits very neatly into many different religious traditions. . . . people seem to have a greater degree of tolerance and acceptance and appreciation for many different religious ways of life other than their own, but including their own. . . . the research and study that I have done on the experience has probably inclined me to a view not all that different from that of the typical NDE experience. In other words, I think that I would share the point of view that I just tried to express as being relatively common for many NDErs.[21]

Ring also admits:

> The view that I have of religion and spiritual matters has been shaped to some considerable degree by the studies that I've made of the NDE and the people that I've come to meet in the course of this work. . . . I feel like one NDEr . . . [who] said, "Every religion has beauty." She somehow felt that she could somehow see into the essential core that unites all religious faiths, however diverse they may seem and however different their actual exoteric doctrines may

be. And I think I feel somewhat similarly.[22]

Regarding heaven and hell, these concepts have been discarded by Ring very much on the basis of his NDE research. "If I were constrained to speak about this," he said during one interview, "I would certainly say I don't believe it's so simple and straightforward as the good go to heaven and the bad go to hell."[23] He elaborates:

> I think you're likely to have an experience where you see yourself as it actually is. . . . You'd probably judge yourself. . . . I think there's a relationship surely as to how we lived here, what we've cultivated in ourselves to what we experience after death, but I wouldn't want to put it in terms of reward/punishment or heaven/hell models. The implications of the NDE does not suggest a heaven and hell model. . . . my understanding of death and what happens after death is very similar to what NDEers would say.[24]

Ring, like Eadie and other NDErs, subscribes to the "life-reviewal" scenario of judgment. "All researchers," he concedes, "have encountered people who've lived less than exemplary lives, yet had very positive experiences, but that doesn't mean they're exempt from paying a price. The 'life review' is the great equalizer."[25]

It should not be assumed from the above quotations that Ring's New Age spirituality is *solely* the result of information gleaned from NDEs. His beliefs have sprung both from his professional studies as well as from his personal experiences.[26] In one interview, he pointed out that his research only confirmed what he had already believed to be true:

> I wasn't like an atheist converted into [sic] a fox-hole doing NDE research. I was already quite convinced that there was something, for lack of a better word, we'll call God. I think the work on the NDE should reinforce that; it maybe deepened my conviction, but it didn't fundamentally change it.[27]

Concerning the identity of "the light" seen by most

NDErs, Ring speculates that it may actually be *"oneself*, in a higher form. . . . a reflection of one's own inherent divine nature and symbolizes the higher self. The light one sees, then, is one's own."[28] This "higher self" is also often referred to by New Agers. They consider it that inner part of everyone which is divine:

> Higher Self. The most spiritual and knowing part of oneself, said to lie beyond the ego, the day-to-day personality or self, and beyond the personal unconscious, and which can be channeled for wisdom and guidance; variations include the *oversoul*, the *superconscious*, the *Atman, Christ* (or *Krishna* or *Buddha*) *Consciousness, the God within,* or *the God Self.*[29]

Ring explains his similar view this way:

> If one can accept the idea of a higher self, it is not difficult to assume that that self—as well as the individual self—is actually an aspect of God, or the Creator, or any such term with which one feels comfortable.[30]

Despite these beliefs, Ring continues to insist: "I don't have a particular religious orientation as such, but I never have, and I don't expect to."[31] This attitude is common among NDErs and those who conduct NDE research. They consistently fail to see that they do indeed have a particular "religious" orientation. Most prefer to define themselves as "spiritual" rather than "religious."[32]

"A lot of people who have this experience go into the helping profession," related one NDE researcher. "They tell us they're not necessarily more religious, but they're a lot more spiritual."[33] Exactly what does "spiritual" mean? It means not holding to exclusivistic claims like those found in Christianity:

> [P]eople by and large tend to have a more universalistic approach toward spirituality. In fact, many people would say that they become less religious in an outward sense—perhaps in a denominational

sense, or in a sense of organized religion—but they become more inwardly spiritual and closer to God.[34]

Such a position, however, is self-defeating because anyone who states that there exists no "one truth" is actually making a "one truth" claim (i.e., "there is no one truth"). By making such an exclusivistic claim, NDErs have by their own definition become "religious" and are no longer "spiritual."

In other words, the only difference between NDErs and other "religious" people is the particular exclusivistic claim being made. Those in the NDE movement label as "religious" anyone who advocates "one true way." They themselves, at the same time however, advocate one true way by saying "there is no one true way." Those promoting this NDE-inspired faith have simply re-categorized their own exclusivistic claim as "spiritual." It is nothing more than word games.

NDEs are fast developing a new pseudo-scientific religion. This fact may have been unconsciously hinted at by Ring when he said, "the thousands of NDErs who have been interviewed are speaking for millions of their silent brethren."[35] In a more blunt statement, Ring theorizes:

> That the NDE should be a catalyst for religious or spiritual awakening is, in view of all we've considered to this point, hardly surprising. . . . NDErs are likely to shift toward a universalistically spiritual orientation. . . . the strongest evidence of NDErs' universalistically spiritual orientation . . . is their belief in the underlying unity of all religions and their desire for a universal religious faith that will transcend the historical divisiveness of the world's great religions. . . . beyond all this, there is still the profound *evolutionary* meaning of NDEs—that NDErs and others who have had similar awakenings may in some way prefigure our own planetary destiny, the next stage of human evolution, the dazzling ascent toward Omega and the conscious reunion with the Divine.[36]

Ring has recently explored the possibility that NDEs and

181

UFOs may in effect be alternate pathways to a similar psychospiritual transformation. In his 1992 book *The Omega Project*, he asks:

> Are NDEs and UFO encounters (whatever UFOs may be!) in effect *alternate pathways* to the same type of psychospiritual transformation, i.e., one that expresses itself in greater awareness of the inter-connectedness and sacredness of all life and necessarily fosters a heightened ecological concern for the welfare of the planet? . . . Could phenomena so vastly different as NDEs and UFO encounters somehow both be expressions emanating from a common source whose intent furthermore is to strive to awaken the human species to a truth it now desperately needs . . . ?[37]

During one speaking engagement, Ring explained exactly what these spiritual transformations promise to bring:

> Near-death experiences collectively represent an evolutionary thrust toward higher consciousness for humanity as a whole. . . . People who have had near-death experiences, as well as many other people whose lives have been transformed by one or more deep spiritual experiences, all of these people as a totality represent in effect a more highly advanced human being. . . . These are people whose consciousness has been flooded with a . . . higher kind of awareness, a higher spiritual illumination. . . . To my thinking, the emergence of this new strain of human being, if this hypothesis is correct, on the planet now, signals a possibility that the dawning of the New Age is indeed upon us.[38]

Bruce Greyson (IANDS cofounder, former IANDS president)

Bruce Greyson, IANDS' second president, has been studying NDEs as far back as the late 1970s and early 1980s when he was an associate of Moody's.[39] He is currently a clinical psychiatrist and associate professor at the University of Connecticut Medical School (Farmington), and serves as chief of research at IANDS. He is also the editor of IANDS' scholarly *Journal of Near-Death Studies*.

Results from Greyson's research basically coincides with Ring's data. He has additionally discovered that "NDErs undergo radical changes in personality, and their significant others—spouses, friends, relatives—confirm these changes."[40] These changes include a greater appreciation for life, higher self-esteem, elevated spirituality, greater ecological sensitivity and planetary concern, and a feeling of being more intuitive (sometimes psychic).[41]

Like Ring, Greyson has departed from the usual skepticism found among those of the medical community. "I think there is a spiritual realm we are often blind to that is liberated by the proximity of death," he concedes. "I think people do have these experiences."[42]

Further insight into Greyson's personal beliefs surfaced when, during a PEOPLE magazine interview, he was asked to explain the current interest in NDEs: "[M]uch of society has lost faith in traditional religion, we need another source to give us values and tell us what virtue is" (emphasis added).[43]

Visions of God, one of several NDE-faith promoting works, helps identify for us the other "source" of values to which Greyson is referring: "Many of our most inspiring and straightforward visions of God, afterlife, and *values for living* have come through near death experiences" (emphasis added).[44]

Given Greyson's reported concerns over "what can be learned" from NDE-inspired "outlooks on life,"[45] it is understandable that he would enumerate in the PEOPLE interview some of these new values that society so desperately needs as replacements for "traditional" religion. "Most near-death experiencers," he explains, "become less conventionally religious and espouse a universal spirituality, saying things like, 'I'm aware of God in everything.' "[46]

The pantheism suggested here by Greyson is more clearly expressed by Barbara Harris, Greyson's personal research assistant, who is herself an NDEr. When Harris "died" from complications after back surgery she, like many NDErs, was pulled through a dark tunnel toward a bright light. "I knew that the light was God," Harris recalls. "It wasn't an old man with a long white beard, though—it was a force, an energy and a love that went through me."[47]

This monistic/pantheistic world view, which consistently emerges from NDEs, appears to be the theology of choice for those in the NDE movement:

> Respondents often claim to be aware of having a very special relationship to this presence which is sometimes understood to be God, and at times is felt to be the higher self of the individual. Very often these two are perceived to be one and the same and people frequently stress that there is, in reality, no separation from God.[48]

> I seem to have a greater awareness of all living things and that we are ALL a part of one another and ultimately a part of a greater consciousness, God.[49]

> I think of God as a tremendous source of energy, like the nucleus of something enormous and that we are all just separate atoms from this nucleus. I think that God is in every one of us; we are God . . . .[50]

> God was me and I was God. I was part of the light and I was one with it. I was not separate. I am not saying that I am a supreme being. I was God, as you are, as everyone is.[51]

It must be noted that Greyson is somewhat unique among most NDE researchers because of his interest in not only the "heavenly" NDEs, but also in the small percentage of "hellish" NDEs that are regularly reported. These negative experiences, which are for understandable reasons often ignored, have motivated him to work closely with Nancy Evans Bush—the current president of IANDS—who is also interested in "hellish" NDEs.

Nancy Evans Bush (IANDS President)

Although she is not a psychiatrist, psychologist or medical doctor, Nancy Evans Bush has been studying NDEs for more than 12 years. She was elected as the fifth president of IANDS in 1991 after the terms of the third and fourth presidents—John Alexander and Elizabeth Fenski—had expired. (Because Alexander and Fenski have not contributed as significantly to NDE research as have their coresearcher, they will not be discussed.)

Bush has done extensive near-death studies, specifically in connection with unpleasant NDEs. As of 1993 she had collected 50 such cases.[52] According to Bush, these "hellish" NDEs fit into one of three categories. The first "resembles a positive experience except that the person has interpreted it in a different way and has often been terrified by the sense of losing control. . . . A person who approaches the light and is so fearful may see it as a reflection of the fires at the gates of hell, instead of seeing it as a radiant light."[53]

A second group of people experience "a great cosmic nothingness. Sensations of being caught in a void, with an accompanying sense of abandonment," she adds, "frequently lead to long-term despair."[54]

Those in the third, and smallest, group "claim that they saw a vision of hell."[55] In some of these latter accounts, "people claim that they have had to observe others being tortured or tormented."[56]

Bush claims to be a Christian.[57] She even has a master's degree in pastoral ministry from St. Joseph's University, West Hartford, Connecticut, and is a member of the United Church of Christ denomination (UCC). The UCC, however, "has a reputation as one of the most socially liberal and active of American church bodies. . . . It is also theologically liberal."[58]

Theologically liberal individuals often deny several major tenets of Christianity including: the Trinity, the deity of Christ, the virgin birth, and the inerrancy/infallibility of Scripture. In order to clear up any doubts about Bush's "Christianity" I conducted an interview with her on August 1, 1994.

"What is your religious background and your position on religion and spiritual beliefs?" I asked.

"I'm a Christian."

Her encouraging answer was soon overshadowed by a clarification: "I certainly am not—and am practically at the opposite poles—of literalist-fundamentalists."

As our conversation continued, Bush grew notably more evasive about her doctrinal views. That is, until I asked, "For your particular denomination, for you yourself even, would you fit into the category of people who would say that Jesus was God in the flesh?"

Apparently, I had struck a nerve. She answered rather forcefully: "No! Absolutely not!"

When I asked Bush about the kind of universalism that comes out of NDEs, she explained to me that "what happens with NDEs is what happens out of any significant kind of spiritual maturation." According to Bush, universalism is a more "mature" level of spirituality than the kind of exclusivistic claims found among fundamentalist Christians.

When it comes to identifying "the light," Bush is much more cautious than are her fellow NDE researchers. She simply doesn't know what it is:

> I've found a very great tolerance for ambiguity which is not shared by a great many people. I don't feel any compelling need to demand that the light stand up and identify itself. I'm perfectly comfortable with the realization with whatever it is, something seems to be happening surrounding the experience which puts people in touch with something, whatever it is, and I don't know what is. We can put theological labels on them, but we may be wrong. It's just not one of my big questions.[59]

My interview with Bush came to a rather abrupt conclusion when one of my questions was simply too straightforward: "Who, or what is God?" After exactly 21 seconds of silence Bush replied, "How does this tie in [with NDEs]?"

I assured the IANDS president that my question was indeed relevant. Eventually she gave an answer, which although it did not express her view of God, clearly alluded to the impersonal shape-shifting "One" of the New Age movement: "Whatever words I put to it [God] will not necessarily fit other people's experience. All of these [NDEs] are intensely subjective experiences. I am no more an authority on what is God than you, or any of the people who will read your book. . . . each of those readers will have either a relationship or a non-relationship with something they consider to be God."

Michael Sabom (IANDS researcher, IANDS first vice-president)

When cardiologist Michael Sabom first read *Life After Life* in 1977, he thought it was "fairly ridiculous."[60] "I was a cardiology fellow down at the University of Florida," he remembers, "at the time and I had not heard of these experiences from my own patients. And so, when I read his [Moody's] book, I thought that he was making up most of it."[61]

Sabom's skepticism quickly deteriorated, however, when he started talking to some of his own patients whom he had resuscitated. Many described similar experiences to those collected by Moody. The discovery prompted him to undertake a five-year study.[62] It became "a benchmark" in NDE research.[63] A September 1988 *Psychology Today* article describes the study:

> [Sabom] examined the NDEs of 116 people, dividing their experiences into three types: autoscopic (an out-of-body experience), transcendental (entry into a "spiritual realm") and experiences that mixed the two. He talked to 32 people who claimed to have observed their own resuscitation by emergency room doctors, and he compared their descriptions with the "educated guesses" of patients who had undergone resuscitation but had not had out-of-body experiences. He found that 23 of 25 patients in the comparison group made major mistakes in describing the resuscitation procedure, while none of the patients claiming out-of-body experiences made a mistake.[64]

The data made clear to Sabom that his original suspicions were wrong.[65] He published his findings in *Recollections of Death: A Medical Investigation*. Prior to its publication, Sabom had been one of those who helped start the Association for the Scientific Study of Near-Death Phenomena—the group which eventually became IANDS. In Sabom's words, "We all [Moody, Ring, Greyson, etc.] met in Charlottesville, Virginia, in the late seventies at Moody's house, and out of that meeting came the idea that we would form an organization whose purpose would be to look into the NDE. That's where IANDS was born."[66]

In a *TIME* magazine interview, Sabom candidly remarked: "Personally, I believe in life after death."[67] He confirmed this to me during an 8/3/94 interview. His belief in the afterlife, however, is not based on his research. "I do believe personally that there is an afterlife," Sabom says, "but that is based upon my Christian religious beliefs and my faith."

Much to my surprise, I found that Sabom is a Christian and a member of the Presbyterian Church in America (a conservative denomination), which makes a firm commitment to the essential beliefs of historic orthodox Christianity primarily through unwavering adherence to the Westminster Confession of Faith and Catechisms.[68]

During our conversation, Sabom affirmed the orthodox doctrines of the Trinity, the virgin birth, the full deity and humanity of Jesus Christ, salvation by grace alone through faith alone, and the personality and deity of the Holy Spirit. He also very clearly stated, "I'm not New Age!"[69]

Sabom agrees that there is a disturbing amount of New Age belief coming out of NDEs. In fact, he expressed frustration at seeing New Agers using his book to support their views:

> I wanted to keep religion out of this in the early eighties, and I wanted to look at it from a medical and scientific standpoint. I didn't want this to become a religious war, but it's become that. And a lot of people are using my book [*Recollections of Death: A Medical Investigation*] to support their New Age beliefs.[70]

Sabom considers NDEs to be near-death experiences rather than *after*-death experiences. In other words, he believes that NDEs are definitely spiritual experiences, but emphatically does not view them as tastes of the afterlife.[71] Exactly what, then, is going on with NDEs? Sabom is not sure. He is in the midst of another study which will soon be published in another book.

Concerning the New Age beliefs which frequently emerge from NDEs and members of IANDS, Sabom makes some valid observations:

> Personally, everybody brings their own bias into the research. That includes me, Ring, Morse, Moody, everybody. . . . When someone is using an experience like the NDE as a reason for their beliefs, you have to question whether they had the belief that preexisted the research. What I feel is that most of the people are bringing their own bias into the research. They're finding something within the research experience that seemingly corresponds with their world view . . . as a way of supporting their world view. And I'm applying that to myself too. . . . to say that anyone is just objectively looking at the NDE with no preconceptions, no presuppositions, no world views is naive. . . . I feel that the near-death experience is a real experience and I feel like we all—regardless of our preconceptions or our presuppositions—we all need to do research in a way that data can be used by anyone for whatever reason they want to use it. There's no such thing as absolutely clean data, but I do think that we need to strive much harder to do research into the NDE which is not encumbered by our own presuppositions and preconceptions. Once we can do that we can talk on a level of "Well, what does your data show; what does my data show?" . . . IANDS is striving toward this kind of approach where you can have differing opinions about the meaning, but you can still interact on the level of data. There's always going to be a majority opinion and a minority opinion. And the majority right now is the universalist opinion. But quite frankly it's because most of

the people doing the research into the field are universalists.[72]

NDE research has long been ignored by Christians. The kind of work Sabom is doing, and the integrity with which he is doing it, indicates that perhaps it is time for him to be joined by other Christian physicians and scientists.

Dr. Melvin Morse (pediatrician)

Dr. Melvin Morse—a pediatrician at Seattle Children's Hospital—began his NDE research approximately 12 years ago. Although not a member of IANDS, he is a regularly featured speaker at IANDS conventions and has been "really influenced by all the IANDS guys."[73] His research is unique in that it focuses on the NDEs of children.

Morse's findings, first published in 1990 as *Closer to the Light: Learning from the Near-Death Experiences of Children*, indicated that children—despite a lack of spiritual training, bias and cultural conditioning—often reported having NDEs. Of course, the children expressed their NDEs in much less sophisticated terms than "I beheld a glorious being of light," or "The peace and contentment were beyond comprehension."

A five-year-old named Jane, for example, drew a picture of "Jesus" that looked remarkably like Santa Claus.[74] Little seven-year-old Kurt, a victim of muscular dystrophy whose heart stopped beating for three minutes, described seeing "a beautiful place with flowers and rainbows."[75] Other children, when talking about the "light" that is so common in NDEs, often say things like: "[T]here were a lot of good things in that light."[76]

In Morse's second book, *Transformed by the Light*, he published data from a study he made of adults who had had NDEs as children. Morse found that each had undergone an emotional and spiritual transformation. They were, among other things, more at peace with life, more willing to help others, less materialistic, and less prone to alcohol or drug addiction than the average American adult. Morse is perhaps the most important NDE researcher to emerge in the last 10 years, especially with regard to Betty Eadie. He wrote the foreword to *Embraced By The Light*. "This book," notes Morse, "is really a textbook of the near-death experience, written as a simple and wonderful story that we can all understand."[77]

His glowing review continues: "Her experience answers questions that people have had for me for years about near-death experiences—questions I have never been able to answer. . . . I realize, after reading Betty's book, that my own life has been changed by it, that I need to reconnect with simple truths that I have always known but have ignored."[78]

During a July 29, 1994, interview with Morse, I learned that the "simple truths" he is referring to in the foreword of Eadie's book are the same ones put forth by New Agers: 1) God is an energy force; 2) all religions are equally valid; and 3) there is no hell. (I additionally found Morse to be the most biased against Christianity. At one point in our interview he actually referred to Billy Graham as "not normal" because Graham is a "Fundamentalist Christian.")

I also learned that Morse penned his foreword to *Embraced By The Light* fully realizing that it contained LDS doctrines. This, however, did not dissuade him from supporting Eadie because he feels that all NDEs are 99 percent a product of the mind. Morse is not saying that NDEs are unreal. He simply believes that they are subjective experiences occurring in response to an objective God, that "God" being the pantheistic One permeating "all that is."

When asked specifically about his "religious" beliefs, Morse responded: "Well, I don't really have any religious beliefs or any spiritual beliefs."[79] Contradicting his assertion, however, were several spiritual *and* religious convictions he went on to espouse during the remainder of our conversation:

> **MORSE** From a personal standpoint, after studying near-death research, I am absolutely convinced of the statement that all of life is interconnected. And I believe that there is some sort of godly glue that unifies the universe. . . . I believe there is some unseen pattern, or force, or God, or whatever you want to call it.
>
> **ABANES** Would it be similar to what is known in

some of the other religions as the chi force, or ki, or prana?

MORSE Sure. I think that that's exactly [it]. Sure. I think that's the exact same thing.

ABANES So there's this—to borrow a phrase from "Star Wars"—Force permeating "all that is?"

MORSE Yeah.

ABANES And that this Force is God?

MORSE Well, I'm gonna say that God is at least that. I don't know what God is. . . . whatever that Force is, I believe it's the light of the near-death experience.

ABANES What is this light? Some say it's Christ. Some say it's Buddha. Some say it's just an energy. What is it *objectively* as opposed to *subjectively*?

MORSE Well, objectively, it's God. It's whatever God is.

ABANES And subjectively it manifests itself to these individuals?

MORSE Oh, sure.

ABANES It does so as what they can most closely identify with?

MORSE Yeah. You see that the best in kids. Because listen to this: a lot of kids see it as a living [school] teacher; a living teacher! So, see what I mean? A living teacher. So, that says it all to me. I've had two or three cases like that. Or, a guy [child] says it's a wizard dressed in white—and he's crazy about Nintendo. This 10-year-old boy says it's a wizard dressed in white who told him, "Struggle and you shall live" [laughs].

ABANES Which is very Nintendo-ish.

MORSE Yeah. Right.

ABANES Would you personally agree with the apparent universalistic type approach to religions and salvation that is usually a common thread throughout NDEs? Basically, discarding the more exclusivistic claims of say, for example, orthodox fundamental Christianity?

MORSE Right. I agree with that. Sure.

ABANES The universalism?

MORSE Sure. But I don't know anything about

religion. So, I wouldn't take *my* word on it. I'd ask some religious type that question. You know who would be great? Tom Harpur. He's a priest. He wrote a super book on near-death experiences. . . . He is, to my knowledge, the only, you know, kind of nor-mal—I'm gonna say normal—religious person who's looked at near-death experiences. Now, I know Billy Graham's talked about them. A lot of people have written books about them. I'm just saying to me it's the only, you know "normal" [book] written by somebody who seems halfway normal.

ABANES So, Billy Graham is not halfway "normal?"

MORSE [long pause] Well, [pause] he's a fundamen-talist Christian. You know, that's for sure. He's ex-treme. I don't think that's unfair to say that he's extreme. I mean, he may be right. I'm not going to judge whether he's right or wrong. I think *he* would admit that he's definitely "one of the few." Whereas a Catholic priest—who Tom Harpur is—is a little more mainstream. That's a fair way to put it [chuckles]. I can see it's gonna come out in your article, now he says [laughs] Billy Graham isn't normal [sustained laughter through next sentence]. No, I don't think he's too normal! [continues to laugh]. But, you know. I've read his books. I'll tell you that much.

ABANES Billy Graham's books?

MORSE Yeah.

ABANES Oh, really?

MORSE Oh, sure. A lot of people are deeply troubled by near-death experiences and they send me his books and stuff. The fundamentalist Christians, you know, they fear near-death experiences. They believe that they're the devil's lie.

ABANES Because of the "angel of light" that appears?

MORSE Yeah. That's Satan.

ABANES Second Corinthians describes how Satan can appear as an angel of light.

MORSE Exactly. . . . I've been on fundamentalist Christian radio stations and I've heard an earful.

ABANES I'm sure you have. And the disturbing thing for them, I think, is the universalistic approach that, in their opinion, relegates Jesus Christ to a position of any other religious teacher.

MORSE Oh, sure. Yeah.

ABANES Speaking of Betty Eadie, how did you get involved with her book?

MORSE She just asked me if I'd write the foreword to it.

ABANES There's been some discussions insofar as the legitimacy of her report because it contains so much Mormon doctrine.

MORSE Well, she's Mormon! What did you think, Richard? [laughs] That she'd have Buddhist teachings?

ABANES Well, that's the thing. Where is there objective reality in these things? Is there, or is there not, spirits waiting to be born? Is there, or is there not, eternal progression? These are the things she says she saw—at least subjectively—in the experience. But where does an objective truth come in here? Is it real?

MORSE Well, that's not a question I can even begin to address. I'm a pediatrician. I think I'll skip that one.

ABANES What about hellish experiences?

MORSE To me they're just cut from the same cloth as the heavenly experience. . . . They're from the "Bible Belt." They're from Nashville, Tennessee. They believe in hell down there.

ABANES You're saying that most of what actually occurs in the NDE comes from the mind?

MORSE Ninety-nine percent of it, I believe. Raymond Moody wrote a whole book on people who see Elvis in their near-death experience. So, there you go.

ABANES Interesting. If NDEs are 99 percent a part of the mind, where does the godlike glue of the universe—the prana, the chi, the ki—come from?

MORSE I believe that we have a specific area of our brain that's devoted to sensing God [right temporal lobe].

ABANES So, when this right temporal lobe kind of "kicks in" we have these spiritual experiences?

MORSE Yeah.

ABANES And we can perceive "God," which is this all pervading energy, or force, that exists?

MORSE Sure. That's my opinion.

Another disturbing aspect of Morse's beliefs is his apparent support of euthanasia. I first suspected that Morse was supportive of such a method of putting dying patients out of their "misery" when I read a 10/14/90 *Rocky Mountain News* article in which he is quoted as saying:

> I used to think I should resuscitate every patient endlessly, but now I think that's wrong. We should stop, tell the family no more can be done, then bring the family in and tell them the patient may well have experiences that will explain death to the family.[80]

Not until I spoke with Morse did I realize how strongly he felt about helping the hopelessly ill move on into the life that awaits them after death (see Appendix B). His NDE studies are intimately linked with his views on euthanasia. To Morse, the "other side" is so much better than "this side" that there is no reason to irrationally hold on to life here if you are suffering.

How does Morse know that what lies beyond death will be pleasant, full of total love and acceptance, and be non-judgmental for everyone? Because, says Morse: "There are definitely people who have come back with the answers to life and death. At least they feel they have and I guess I think they have come back with the answer—because it rings so true to me and it's such a simple and prosaic answer."[81]

What It All Means

Have people really come back from being dead with glimpses of eternity? Can their stories be trusted? What about the NDE-inspired doctrines which so blatantly contradict Scripture?

Christians must wrestle with such questions, but these are not the points with which many in the NDE movement are concerned. Their main purpose is to promote an all-inclusive gospel of love, acceptance, and universalism which leaves no room for the God of the Bible.

"For the time will come," said Paul the apostle, "when men will not put up with sound doctrine. Instead, to suit their own desires, they will gather around them a great number of teachers to say what their itching ears want to hear. They will turn their ears away from the truth and turn aside to myths" (2 Timothy 4:3–4).

Today, there are indeed new teachers being raised up by the forces of darkness. They come bearing promises of eternal life regardless of what one believes. Ironically, their calling card is death.

ENDNOTES

[1] Lueders, Beth. *Clarity*, "Out of Body or Out of Your Mind," May/June, p. 32.

[2] n.a. IANDS pamphlet, p. 3.

[3] Ibid.

[4] Genova, Amy Sunshine. *McCall's*, "The Near-Death Experience," 2/88 p. 104.

[5] IANDS pamphlet, op. cit., pp. 3–4.

[6] Author's 7/20/94 interview with IANDS.

[7] Ibid.

[8] Ring, Kenneth. Author's 7/22/94 interview with Ring.

[9] Bush, Nancy Evans. Publicity Letter in IANDS Information Packet, n.d., p. 1.

[10] Lueders, op. cit., p. 31.

[11] Ring, op. cit.

[12] Constable, George, ed. *Psychic Voyages*, Mysteries of the Unknown Series, p. 72.

[13] Yamamoto, J. Isamu. *Christian Research Journal*, "The Near-Death Experience," Spring 1992, pp. 30–31.

[14] Ibid.

[15] Ring, Kenneth. *Heading Toward Omega*, p. 226.

[16] Ring, author's 7/22/94 interview, op. cit.

[17] Constable, op. cit., p. 77.

[18] Ibid.

[19] Ibid., p. 73.

[20] Ibid.

[21] Ring, author's 7/22/94 interview, op. cit.

[22] Ibid.

[23] Kee, Christine A. and Nancy Pridmore. *Plato's Cave*, "Near-Death Experiences: An Interview with Kenneth Ring," p. 3.

[24] Ibid., pp. 3–4.

[25] Genova, op. cit., p. 106.

[26] Ring, author's 7/22/94 interview, op. cit.

[27] Kee and Pridmore, op. cit., p. 1.

[28] Ring, Kenneth. *Life at Death: A Scientific Investigation of the Near-Death Experience*, pp. 240–241.

[29] Klimo, Jon. *Channeling*, p. 347.

[30] Ring, *Life*, op. cit., p. 241.

[31] Ring, author's 7/22/94 interview, op. cit.

[32] Genova, Amy Sunshine. *Denver Post*, "Near-Death Experiences Radically Transform Lives," 9/23/88, p. 1F; cf. *McCalls*, "The Near-Death Experience," by Amy Sunshine Genova, February 1988, p. 105.

[33] Pearson, Mike. *Rocky Mountain News*, "Into the Light," 3/15/89, p. 49.

[34] Ring, author's 7/22/94 interview, op. cit.

[35] Constable, op. cit, p. 77.

[36] Ring, *Heading*, op. cit., pp. 144–145, 162, 269.

[37] Ring, Kenneth. *The Omega Project*, pp. 11–12.

[38] Ring, Kenneth. Charlottesville Conference as quoted in *Otherworld Journeys: Accounts of Near-Death Experience in Medieval and Modern Times* by Carol Zaleski, pp.107–108.

[39] Somerville, Barbara. *Denver Post*, "Brushes With Death Cast New Light On Life," 5/13/90, p. 10.

[40] Mauro, James. *Psychology Today*, "Bright Lights, Big Mystery," July/August 1992, p. 82.

[41] Ibid.

[42] Longley, Anne. *PEOPLE*, "A Glimpse Beyond," 8/1/94, p. 44.

[43] Ibid.

[44] Vincent, Ken R. *Visions of God*, back cover.

[45] Mauro, op. cit.

[46] Longley, op. cit.

[47] Ebert, Alan. *Redbook*, "A Glimpse of Heaven," July 1991, p. 89.

[48] Grey, Margot. *Return from Death: An Exploration of the Near-Death Experience*, pp. 76–77 as quoted in *Near Death or Deception?*, an unpublished manuscript by Philip J. Porvaznik, University of South Florida, p. 6.

[49] Ring, *Heading*, op. cit., p. 220.

[50] Ibid., p. 151.

[51] Zaleski, Carol. *OtherWorld Journeys*, p. 126.

[52] Rawlings, Maurice. *To Hell and Back*, p. 88.

[53] Underwood, Nora. MACLEAN'S, "Between Life and Death," 4/20/92, p. 36.

[54] Ibid.

[55] Ibid., pp. 36–37.

[56] Ibid., p. 37.

[57] Ring, author's 7/22/94 interview.

[58] Melton, J. Gordon. Encyclopedia of American Religions, p. 349.

[59] Bush, Nancy Evans. Author's 8/1/94 interview with Bush.

[60] Sabom, Michael. Author's 8/3/94 interview with Sabom.

[61] Ibid.

[62] Ibid.

[63] Perry, Paul. *Psychology Today*, "Brushes with Death," September 1988, p. 14.

[64] Ibid.

[65] Wallis, Claudia. TIME, "Going Gently into That Good Night," February 8, 1982, p. 79.

[66] Sabom, op. cit.

[67] Wallis, op. cit.

[68] Melton, op. cit., p. 338.

[69] Sabom, op. cit.

[70] Ibid.

[71] Ibid.

[72] Ibid.

[73] Morse, Melvin. Author's 7/29/94 interview with Morse.

[74] Krier, Beth Ann. *Los Angeles Times*, "Near-Death Visions," 9/18/90, p. E6.

[75] Jones, Verna Noel. *Rocky Mountain News*, "Closer to the Light," 10/14/90, p. 20M.

[76] Ibid.

[77] Eadie, Betty. *Embraced By The Light*, foreword by Melvin Morse, p. ix.

[78] Ibid, pp. x, xii.

[79] Morse, op. cit.

[80] Jones, op. cit., p. 21M.

[81] Krier, op. cit.

CHAPTER 12

November 19, 1973

Worrying about questions like, "Is every single word of Betty Eadie's book true?" is missing the point.

— Dr. Melvin Morse, pediatrician[1]

"Why should anyone believe your story?" I asked Betty Eadie.

"I don't know that they should," she replied.

Before I could formulate a response, Eadie continued:

> I would not want anyone to take my book and think that it is the gospel because it is not. It's an experience and we all perceive things the best way we know how from our own perception. I caution anyone that reads any book to read it, receive what you can, if it is good, then accept it. If it is not, then reject it.[2]

This sentiment goes well with Eadie's current conviction about not wanting to proselytize. Her feelings might best be summarized in this way: If you believe what I say, great! If you don't, that's fine too. I'm only *sharing* an experience, not trying to *prove* one.[3]

Despite Eadie's contention that she is simply "sharing" an experience,[4] it cannot be denied that she is actually converting many people to a specific set of doctrines about God,

Jesus, salvation, heaven, hell, the nature of man, sin and forgiveness.

Anyone else promoting such things would quickly be identified as a religious figure. Eadie, however, is not so easily classified because she is not a doctrinal teacher per se. Is she someone, then, who is truly just sharing an experience in the same way someone would talk about a vacation? Definitely not. But by saying that her book, her many talk show appearances and her lectures are merely vehicles for sharing, Eadie places herself in a sort of religious no-man's land.

A number of modern-day promoters of "spiritual" beliefs do this same thing. Shirley MacLaine, for example, maintains: "I'm not proselytizing—I'm sharing."[5] Henry Gordon of the Committee for the Scientific Investigation of Claims of the Paranormal (CSICOP) makes some keen observations about MacLaine, which can appropriately be applied to Eadie:

> To proselytize is to convert or attempt to convert someone from one belief to another. Can someone who spreads her beliefs by writing books, conducting seminars, . . . going on countless talk shows . . . really claim that she is not proselytizing? Let's look at the definition of the word "sharing." To share is to apportion something, to divide and distribute. True, Shirley is distributing something. But when you do it for a price, it's called "selling," isn't it?[6]

Eadie's "sharing" mode of operation yields her several benefits. First, anyone offended by religious people who proselytize will have no problem with Eadie. She is just "sharing."

Second, those who *are* religiously/spiritually inclined (i.e., Christians, Mormons, New Agers, etc.) will more readily accept Eadie's story: 1) because of its religious overtones; and 2) because it sounds so similar to doctrines they already believe.

Third, individuals looking for spiritual answers will be drawn to Eadie because she does nothing more than place before them a mixed plate of spiritual "truths" from which they can pick and choose what they desire without feeling pressured to accept any of them.

Eadie's unthreatening method of spreading doctrines further provides a shield against critics who might call upon her to prove that she died. As long as she avoids trying to *convince* people of her NDE, she never has to document her death.

Missing Medical Records

About the only thing missing from Eadie's story—aside from doctrines consistent with her professed Christianity—is concrete evidence supporting the claim that she died. None of Eadie's medical records have ever been made public. When asked during one interview if she would someday make such records available for inspection, she replied, "No, I doubt it."[7]

In response to a similar question posed by "American Journal," Eadie adamantly stated that she would never show them. "Nor would [I] be subject to hypnosis," she continued. "Nor would I be subject to a [polygraph test] . . . I don't need credibility. I'm not trying to prove my experience, I'm sharing it."[8]

Eadie's unwillingness to document her death may stem from the fact that there exist no medical records supporting her claims. In a PEOPLE magazine article she admitted: "The exact length of time I was dead and whatnot were not documented, so I don't have those facts."[9]

But surely there must be some "facts" in Eadie's possession which could verify a few aspects of her story. For example, the name of the doctor who performed the surgery which led to Eadie's NDE would be helpful. Eadie, however, also refuses to divulge this information.

When interviewed by ABC's "20/20," Eadie gave two completely different reasons for why she would not reveal her physician's name. She first told the investigative news program that she did not want to injure his reputation. Then, Eadie said her doctor had died.[10]

Tom Britton, Eadie's executive assistant, gives yet another reason for silence: "Hospital records and doctors' names are very personal to Betty. She also feels that people who need proof of her story, even if they get the proof, won't accept it."[11]

These reasons for not producing medical records stand in conflict to page 132 of *Embraced By The Light*, which relates how Eadie supposedly met with her doctor five years after "dying" in order to find out if he knew anything about what had happened during the night in question. She did not go back to the physician for *her* peace of mind. Instead, she went because "her friends" wanted more information.[12]

If Eadie had no problem seeking verification of her death for friends in 1978, why is such verification now unimportant? Why is documentation supporting her claims now suddenly not worth producing for the general public? It may be that Eadie herself has become indifferent to what her medical records indicate. "How I died," she confesses, "has never been of interest to me, and it isn't even interesting to me now. I almost feel like I'm being blasphemous by speculating as to whether I died, or how I died because I was told when I was there by Jesus Christ Himself that I had died."[13]

In other words, Eadie *knows* she died because of what she was told during her NDE. "I didn't assume I was dead," she said during one talk show, "I was told that I had died by the guardian angels and Jesus Christ, who of course I believed."[14]

Alternate Explanations

Eadie's test for whether or not her NDE really happened is twofold. First, she presupposes that her subjective experience was absolutely real. Next, she validates that experience from within the experience itself. This is known as arguing in a circle. It's as reliable a way of knowing reality as believing a dishonest salesman who tells you he is honest. After all, he says he is telling you the truth.

What if her NDE was an hallucination? Eadie has admitted to having hallucinated before while hemorrhaging during the birth of her second child.[15] How does she know that her now famous NDE was not a similar hallucination? If it was an hallucination, then the being of light along with the guardian angels who spoke to her could have been hallucinations as well. Hence, the answers they gave her about the reality of the NDE were also unreal, which would in turn mean that the whole experience never happened.

Eadie explains away this scenario by once more turning to the NDE itself. "When I was in that state of being, death," she recounts, "my awareness was heightened and the colors were more real."[16] Should colors be the criteria by which Eadie measures such a life-changing event, especially when the experience affects so many other people, and when there is such a strong possibility that the NDE was an exceptionally clear hallucination?

Pages 27–28 of *Embraced By The Light* indicate that at the time of her death, Eadie was in a trancelike hypnagogic state. Eadie, a registered hypnotherapist, even describes an early part of her experience as "almost hypnotic" (p. 37). Many hypnotherapists can place themselves in hypnotic trances. This is significant because according to the *Encyclopedia of Occultism and Parapsychology*, the hypnotic trance, when frequently induced, "may gradually become spontaneous."[17] The *New Age Almanac* chapter on "Hypnosis and Self-Hypnosis" comments on the image vividness achievable during such a hypnotic state: "A person in a deeper trance, when told a story, can hardly be persuaded afterward that the story was not in fact a real series of events."[18]

The wide range of religious doctrines found in Eadie's experience could have resulted from the broad scope of her religious training. As Eadie said during one talk show, "I was raised in a 'Heinz 57' religious background: Catholic, Methodist, you name it."[19] Her mind could easily have produced a complex hallucination into which all of these beliefs were incorporated.

What if Eadie's NDE was a demonic illusion brought on by demonic forces for the purpose of spreading false doctrines? Everything in it would be false: the being of light would not be Jesus (Eadie has admitted that the being of light did *not* identify itself as Jesus, she just "knew" it was Jesus);[20] the heavenly realm she saw would be a fictitious setting; her life review would be a ruse to destroy belief in a future judgment; and so on. If this is what transpired, Eadie could be believing a demonic deception based on affirmations given to her by the very demonic entities that produced the delusion.

A Non-*Fiction Bestseller?*

Betty Eadie insists that she could not have possibly conjured up her story.[21] But why would it be so impossible for her to make up such a tale? Many fiction books contain scenes just as incredible as those found in *Embraced By The Light.* Frank Peretti's *This Present Darkness* is but one example of a popular fiction novel with portions closely matching sections of Eadie's "*non*-fiction" bestseller:

This Present Darkness	*Embraced By The Light*
The moment their feet touched down, the light from their clothes and bodies began to fade. . . . Save for their towering stature they appeared as two ordinary men, one trim and blond, the other built like a tank. . . . Golden belts had become like dark leather, their scabbards were dull copper. . . . They passed quickly through the walls of the church. . . . Inside they found a contingent of warriors already gathered. . . . these were the mighty warriors, the powerful warrior. . . . Armoth . . . whose war cry and fierce countenance	[T]here are other types of angels, including a type called "Warring Angels." It was shown to me that their purpose is to do battle for us against Satan and his angels. . . . there are times when the Warring Angels are necessary to protect us . . . . I saw that they are giant men, muscularly built, with wonderful countenance . . . . They were actually dressed like warriors, in head dress and armor, and I saw that they moved more swiftly than other angels. . . . they

(continued on next page)

This Present Darkness	Embraced By The Light
had often been enough to send the enemy fleeing . . . . Guilo and Armoth had once battled the demon lords . . . and personally guarded a family of missionaries. . . . No warrior . . . could fight as Tal could; no demon could outmaneuver or outspeed him . . . (pp. 43–44).	suddenly rushed off on some mission (pp. 90–91).

Eadie's book also reflects distinctive characteristics of stories previously told by others. One "experience" recounted by Elisabeth Kübler-Ross in the late 1970s sounds very much like an experience described in *Embraced By The Light*:

Kübler-Ross	Eadie
[A]s I focused on it, it turned into a lotus-flower bud. . . . it opened up into the most beautiful lotus flower, . . . and as the flower opened, its absolute fullness in this life was totally present. . . . the flower was full and open. The vibrations stopped, and the million molecules, including me . . . fell into one piece. It was like a million pieces	. . . I noticed a rose near me. . . . I could actually see it growing. As it developed before my eyes, my spirit was moved, and I wanted to experience its life, to step into it and feel its spirit . . . . I seemed to be able to see down into it. . . . I felt the rose's presence around me, as if I were actually inside and part of the flower. I experi-

(continued on next page)

Kübler-Ross	Eadie
fell into one, and I was part of that one. And I finally thought, "I'm okay because I'm part of all this."[22]	enced it as if I *were* the flower. . . . I felt God in the plant, in me. . . . We were all one! . . . being one with everything else, was so great that I will cherish it *forever.*[23]

Did Eadie really become one with a flower during her NDE? Or did she take Kübler-Ross' experience and make it her own? Only Eadie knows, and as we have seen, she has not always been exactly forthcoming with all the facts. Then, again, perhaps her memories have not always coincided.

We have also seen that the doctrines contained in *Embraced By The Light* are unbiblical. Eadie's entire NDE, in fact, stands in direct contrast to what Scripture teaches. But as significant as this may be for Bible-believing Christians, it is meaningless to those who do not accept the Bible as authoritative.

Even these individuals, however, must face a pointed question that is relevant to both Christians and nonchristians alike. Did anything at all happen to Betty Eadie during the night of November 19, 1973? In the absence of medical records and/or testimony from attending physicians, a careful examination of Eadie's story itself may yield an answer.

The Experience

An early 1993 interview with Eadie, published shortly after the release of *Embraced By The Light*, reads: "Eadie's book tells of dying for possibly *up to two hours* . . ." (emphasis added).[24] By mid-1993, however, Eadie's NDE time had grown to nearly five hours.[25] *Embraced By The Light* gives neither figure. It only relates how, after an unspecified length of time in heaven, Eadie came back to life.

A four-hour time measurement of her NDE has also been advanced based upon an event which accompanied Eadie's return from the dead. Page 125 of her book indicates that soon after entering her body she fell asleep: "I don't know how long I slept. When I opened my eyes again it was 2 a.m. It had been over four hours since my death."

Many have interpreted this to mean that Eadie remained dead for more than four hours. She herself has publicly claimed this.[26] But according to *Embraced By The Light*, Eadie did not look at the clock when she returned from the spirit world. She saw the time when she woke up from the sleep into which she had fallen *after* coming back to life, not *as* she came back to life. Consequently, she has no way of knowing whether her NDE itself lasted four hours or four minutes.

Eadie admits this on page 125 of *Embraced By The Light* when, in reference to the same four hours, she states: "How much of that time I had spent in the spirit world I did not know, but four hours didn't seem nearly long enough for all that had happened to me."

How can Eadie state in her book that she does not know how long she was dead, while at the same time claim in newspaper interviews and on television talk shows that she was dead for four hours?

A plausible explanation for what happened to Eadie is that she began having her NDE (or whatever it may have been) at 9:30 p.m. It lasted for only a brief period of time, after which she awoke. At this point she did not look at the clock, but instead fell asleep, only to reawaken some four hours later, at which time she saw that it was 2 a.m. In reality, Eadie's extended NDE may have been a relatively short *non-NDE* event (i.e., a detailed dream or an exceptionally vivid hallucination).

Unanswered Questions

Pages 133–134 of *Embraced By The Light* recount how Eadie's physician told her that she had hemorrhaged and subsequently died while *left alone* during the nurses' night shift change. He also said that because she had been unattended, they did not know exactly how long she had been dead. How, then, did Eadie's doctor know she had died if she was left alone?

Other questions surround Eadie's "return" to life. According to a June 1993 *American Bookseller* magazine article, Eadie claims that "doctors were with her when she regained consciousness."[27] This is confirmed by an Ogden *Standard-Examiner* interview with Eadie which states that she remained dead until she was "found and revived."[28]

But *Embraced By The Light* indicates that Eadie was alone when she came back to life (pp. 123–125). She even fell asleep until 2 a.m. When she awoke, Eadie maintains, "I didn't know if any medical action had been taken to revive me, or even if anyone had been in to see me" (p. 125). Was Eadie revived by her doctor? Was he, or was he not, with her when she regained consciousness? If her doctor was *not* with her, as *Embraced By The Light* indicates, then how could he have known she died?

In contrast to page 125 (which indicates Eadie was alone when she "came back to life"), page 134 suggests there were many people in Eadie's room: "The doctor and nurses worked on me, giving me an injection, more medication, and I.V.s through the rest of the morning." Again, was Eadie alone when her spirit returned to her body or not? Was Eadie "found and revived" or not?

What did Betty Eadie experience during the night of November 19, 1973? Was it a true near-*death* experience? If Eadie is not fabricating the whole story, she and millions of others could be buying into nothing more than either an extremely vivid hallucination or an illusion created by the powers of darkness. Adding to the possibility that Eadie's NDE never happened is an apparent disregard for all objective ways to test the nature of the experience (i.e., Scriptures, medical records, a physician's testimony, etc.).

Conclusion

Embraced By The Light does not seek to tackle global issues. Nor does it try to resolve complex social dilemmas like racism, famine or crime. Eadie's book does not even attempt to make a distinction between right and wrong or truth and error. Its purpose is much simpler: to tell a story through which people can receive comfort, hope, peace and love.

Some portions of Eadie's account seem tailor-made for this

purpose. Page 83, for instance, says that if our deaths are traumatic "the spirit quickly leaves the body, sometimes even before death occurs. If a person is in an accident or fire . . . their spirit may be taken from their body before they experience much pain." Who would not want to believe this, especially if a loved one had died under similar circumstances?

But just because something sounds wonderful does not make it real or true. There must be something beyond our deceptive emotions and fallible thoughts by which we can determine what is true. For Christians, this objective standard for measuring truth is the Bible.

Scripture, in the words of Paul the apostle, is "useful for teaching, rebuking, correcting and training in righteousness so that the man of God may be thoroughly equipped for every good work" (2 Timothy 3:16–17).

Even Betty Eadie recognizes the importance of God's Word. During a WMUZ interview, Christian radio talk show host Al Kresta asked Eadie: "You are open to comparing your experience to what is in Scripture?"

She replied, "Oh, definitely."

"Scripture would remain authoritative?" Kresta continued. Eadie answered, "It is authoritative."[29]

Previous chapters have shown that Eadie's beliefs are not in line with the Bible. If she is really interested in truth, she will follow through with her words and compare her experience with Scripture, which is, as she herself has said, "authoritative."

It has also been demonstrated that Eadie, for some reason, feels it is unnecessary to be upfront about where many of her doctrines come from (i.e., Mormonism). This, too, must be amended—if only for the sake of her own integrity.

During a "20/20" interview she remarked: "I'm not that bold of a person to tell such a story if it were not true. I would be jeopardizing my position there in that beautiful place if I were to lie to you."[30]

ENDNOTES

[1] Morse, Melvin. Author's 7/29/94 interview with Morse.

[2] Eadie, Betty. Author's 1/25/94 interview with Eadie.

[3] Ho, Vanessa. *Seattle Times.* "Brush with Death Puts Her in the Publishing Spotlight," 6/27/93, p. L3.

[4] Price, Kathie. *The Arizona Republic,* "Visiting Death: Woman Tells of Glimpse of Paradise," 3/13/93, p. B6.

[5] MacLaine, Shirley. As quoted in *Channeling into the New Age* by Henry Gordon, p. 139.

[6] Gordon, Henry. *Channeling into the New Age,* p. 139.

[7] Eadie, op. cit.

[8] Eadie, Betty. "American Journal" program on KCAL, 2/94.

[9] Jerome, Jim. PEOPLE, "Heaven Can Wait," p. 81.

[10] Eadie, Betty. "20/20" program on ABC, 5/13/94.

[11] Britton, Tom. Author's 1/94 interview with Britton.

[12] Eadie, Betty. *Embraced By The Light,* p. 132.

[13] Eadie, "20/20," op. cit.

[14] Eadie, Betty. "Leeza" program on NBC, 6/13/94.

[15] Viotti, Vicki. *The Honolulu Advertiser,* " 'Embraced By The Light' Author Puts Accent on Afterlife," 6/13/94, p. B4.

[16] Ibid.

[17] Shepard, Leslie A. *Encyclopedia of Occultism and Parapsychology,* Vol. 3, p. 1370.

[18] Melton, J. Gordon, Jerome Clark, and Aidan A. Kelly. *New Age Almanac,* p. 57.

[19] "The Oprah Winfrey Show," 1/3/94, (reaired 8/3/94).

[20] Ibid.

[21] Miller, Leslie. *USA Today,* "Betty Eadie, Shedding 'Light' on Her Visit to Heaven," 8/12/93, p. 5D.

[22] Nietzke, Ann. *Human Behavior* (1977), "The Miracle of Kübler-Ross" as reprinted in *Cosmopolitan,* 2/80, p. 210.

[23] Eadie, *Embraced,* op. cit., pp. 80–81.

[24] Phillips, Valerie. [Ogden] *Standard-Examiner,* "Author Shares Love of Life After Death in an Embrace," 3/6/93, n.p.

[25] Perlah, Jeffrey. *American Bookseller,* "An Amazing First-Time Success Story," June 1993, p. 64.

[26] Ibid.

[27] Ibid.

[28] Phillips, op. cit.

[29] WMUZ 3/3/94 taped interview with Al Kresta.

[30] Eadie, Betty. "20/20" program, op. cit.

POSTSCRIPT

Gold Leaf Press
Strikes Again

Gold Leaf Press is now able to produce more books with the proceeds from *Embraced By The Light*. On page 189 of the August 8, 1994, issue of *Publishers Weekly*, Gold Leaf advertised its four newest releases: *Nobody Don't Love Nobody*; *Healing Hearts*; *The Burning Within* (coauthored by Curtis Taylor) and *Leading the Charge* (a biography of Mormon Senator Orrin Hatch). At the bottom of the four-book advertisement appears the following: "Watch for the Special gift edition of *Embraced By The Light*, available for the Fall and Christmas 1994 season from Gold Leaf Press."

As previously noted, Gold Leaf Press is the national marketing division of the Mormon-owned and operated Aspen Books of Murray, Utah. It is well-known to Latter-day Saints as a publisher of Mormon works. This, of course, is not mentioned in the nationally circulated *Publisher's Weekly*. Gold Leaf's full page spread simply reads: "GOLD LEAF PRESS."

Something quite different, however, appears in a recent issue of *IMPRESSIONS*, an informational magazine produced by Deseret Books, which is owned by the Mormon Church. (The magazine's purpose is to inform Mormons about "LDS authors, artists, and products.")[1] This periodical's advertisements for Gold Leaf's new releases do not simply say "Gold

Leaf Press." They read: "Aspen/Gold Leaf" (see photo section).[2]

By linking "Aspen" with Gold Leaf Press, Mormons are alerted to the fact that Gold Leaf's books are written and produced by fellow members of The Church of Jesus Christ of Latter-day Saints. It is unfortunate that the rest of the American public is not given the same information. Gold Leaf Press has certainly found a way to mine its gold.

ENDNOTES

[1] n.a. *IMPRESSIONS*, back cover.

[2] Ibid., pp. 3, 5.

Appendix A

Embraced By The Light:
Which Version Do You Have?

It has been demonstrated that in the predominantly Mormon state of Utah a high degree of publicity about Eadie's LDS membership accompanied the initial release of *Embraced By The Light.* It has also been shown that her book contains a significant amount of Mormon doctrine. What has not been discussed is how certain portions of nationally distributed books were changed, presumably, to be more marketable to non-Mormons.

For example, an explicit reference to Mormonism's "Heavenly Father"—as well as a suggestion of our relationship to him as sexually-begotten, literal, spirit children—was replaced with more generic terminology. In the following comparison, the highlighted text was edited out of the national version:

Embraced By The Light (Utah Version)	*Embraced By The Light* (National Version)
We were with God, and we knew that he *was our Heavenly Father and* that we were *literally* his *spirit* children (p. 47, emphasis added).	We were with God, and we knew that he created us, that *we were his very own children* (p. 47, emphasis added).

217

Also removed from page 47 of nationally distributed versions was a reference to Jesus being a "personage" separate from the Father. This may seem trivial, but describing Jesus as a "personage" is classically Mormon. Joseph Smith Jr., the founder of Mormonism, said: "I have always declared God to be a distinct *personage*, Jesus Christ a separate and distinct *personage* from God the Father, and that the Holy Ghost was a distinct *personage* and a spirit: and these three constitute three distinct *personages* and three Gods" (emphasis added).[1]

Smith's grandnephew, Joseph Fielding Smith, said: "The vision of Joseph Smith made it clear that the Father and the Son are separate *personages*, having bodies as tangible as the body of man" (emphasis added).[2]

Bruce McConkie puts it this way: "Three glorified, exalted, and perfected *personages* comprise the *Godhead.* . . . each God in the Godhead is a *personage*, separate and distinct from each of the others . . . ."[3]

Eadie was communicating a very specific doctrine to her fellow Mormons by using the word "personage" (i.e., denial of the Trinity in favor of Joseph Smith's teachings on God's nature). For non-Mormons, however, the word "personage" would not have been appropriate. Consequently, it was removed:

Embraced By The Light (Utah Version)	*Embraced By The Light* (National Version)
Also, Jesus Christ was there. I understood, to my surprise, that he was a separate *personage* from God . . . (p. 47, emphasis added).	Also, Jesus Christ was there. I understood, to my surprise, that Jesus was a separate *being* from God . . . (p. 47, emphasis added).

Similarly significant changes also appear on pages 35 and 52, but the most noticeable modification is found on page 95. The text deals with the controversial issue of abortion, which Mormons (and Christians) strongly condemn.

The current version of *Embraced By The Light* intimates

that abortion is acceptable, although "contrary to that which is natural" (p. 95). Eadie says prebirth babies are merely bodies waiting for a spirit's arrival from heaven. Each spirit living in the preearth life, she says, can choose exactly when it wants to enter its unborn body.

Tom Britton, Eadie's executive assistant, told me in a January 1994 interview that Eadie feels abortion is "not sin at all."[4] He further told me that during an abortion, a "baby" is not really aborted. Only a spiritless body, which is waiting for a spirit to come to inhabit it, is removed. As Eadie writes, "It [a spirit] knows that the body *was to be* his . . ." (p. 95).

When I asked Britton if Eadie was pro-choice, he said he preferred describing her as "pro-free agency." But this can only mean that Eadie is indeed pro-choice because Mormons define "free agency" as one's personal God-given right and ability to choose between good and evil.[5]

Regarding the ramifications of abortion, Eadie believes that the spirit simply feels "a sense of rejection and sorrow," but that it also feels compassion for the mother knowing that "she made a decision based on the knowledge she had" (p. 95). Up-to-date copies of *Embraced By The Light* are consistent with a politically correct stand. But early Utah-issued copies of the book bring out a much more definable position against abortion.

These versions, for instance, call an unborn baby a "child" whereas later versions speak of the baby as just a body which is entirely separate from the spirit "coming into the body." Additionally, an unborn spirit is referred to as a "he" in first-run copies, but as an "it" in subsequent books. Several other alterations have been made as well. One entire sentence, in fact, on how the unborn spirit feels compassion for the mother who "made a decision based on the knowledge she had," is nowhere in early copies sold to Mormons.

What makes these changes so damaging to Eadie's credibility is that she prefaces her vastly differing explanations about abortion by saying: "Abortion, *I was told* . . ." (emphasis added). It appears that Eadie was "told" two very different things—one fairly strong; the other, markedly soft:

Embraced By The Light (Utah Version)	*Embraced By The Light* (National Version)
Abortion, I was told, is an act against that child. The spirit feels an immediate and devastating rejection. He knows that the body was to be his, whether it was conceived out of wedlock or was handicapped or was only strong enough to live a few hours; but now it has been taken from him. What happens to that spirit, or how it is healed, I don't know (p. 95).	Abortion, I was told, is contrary to that which is natural. The spirit coming into the body feels a sense of rejection and sorrow. It knows that the body was to be his, whether it was conceived out of wedlock or was handicapped or was only strong enough to live a few hours. But the spirit also feels compassion for its mother, knowing that she made a decision based on the knowledge she had (p. 95).

All copies of *Embraced By The Light* currently being sold, including those being distributed in Utah, are now consistent with the National Version. What was Eadie really "told" during her NDE? Was she told anything? Did she even *have* an NDE? The public may never know.

ENDNOTES

[1] Smith, Joseph. *Documentary History of the Church*, 6:474.

[2] Smith, Joseph Fielding. *Doctrines of Salvation*, 1:2.

[3] McConkie, Bruce. *Mormon Doctrine*, p. 319.

[4] Britton, Tom. Author's 1/94 interview with Britton.

[5] McConkie, op. cit., p. 26.

Appendix B

NDEs: A Road to Euthanasia

In chapter 11 of this book we briefly mentioned Dr. Melvin Morse's apparent sympathetic view of euthanasia. To Morse, the information coming out of NDEs legitimizes allowing a patient to, *in some instances*, die. According to Morse, there are already "many cases of euthanasia going on all the time" and we never hear about them. "Patients are allowed to die routinely," revealed Morse. "Patients are given medicines to die routinely, but it's handled in a very personal, and a very private way, with a lot of respect and dignity, and everyone knows what's going on." The following is an edited transcript of our July 29, 1994 interview.

MORSE I think if people paid attention to near-death experiences it would do more to cut health care costs in this country than any—than *any*—health care plan.

ABANES How so?

MORSE Thirty to 60 percent of the health care dollar is spent in the last 24 hours of life.

ABANES Are you serious?

MORSE Yeah. Isn't that amazing? And why do you think we do it? Well, we do it because we're afraid of death. People have the conceit that this medicine, this technology, is actually doing something. And it's very well documented in the medical literature that it's not doing anything. . . . I think it's pretty well accepted within the medical community that this

money is a waste of money. It doesn't prolong life
. . . . I want to make sure I'm being clear about something because people often misunderstand this point
. . . . I am saying that we should spend as much
money as possible to save life. If we have to spend a
million dollars, that's great. . . . But what I'm telling
you is money, that does *not* save a life—under any
circumstances—that doesn't prolong *meaningful* life
30 seconds. That's what I'm saying.

ABANES How do we know where we come back
from that line of death where we say: "Hey, this is
now a waste of money. Let them go"?

MORSE To be candid, I don't think we'll ever be able
to do that. I think that's why we're in the current
state that we're in because we can't do what you just
said. It's just too hard. *But* nevertheless, that point—
although an important one—interestingly enough, I
do not believe dominates the decision-making
process. I think there are relatively few cases which
are of the nature that you described. . . . I quote [in
my article] a woman named Susan Bratton. She's an
intensive care specialist at the Children's Hospital
. . . . Her statement is that only a handful of patients
fit the category that you just said. Most of what we
do, we do as a sense of ritual. As a sense of *irrational*
medical use. We do it because we *can* do it. If you ex-
clude the one in a thousand chances, or the one in a
million chances of living—let's say you excluded
every ethical dilemma. Let's say we just took the position, "Hey, if this is a borderline call, then we'll always err on the side of life." We'll eliminate any case
in which we can't decide whether it should be today,
or tomorrow, or the next day—even so, 99 percent of
the cases are incredibly clear-cut. And that is, we
shouldn't be doing it at all.

ABANES So, you're saying that when a person
reaches a point where it's *obvious*—

MORSE [interrupting] Yeah.

ABANES [continuing] . . . that extraordinary
measures would prolong life for only another,
whatever amount of hours—

222

MORSE [interrupting] Yes.

ABANES [continuing] Just forget it, and let it ride?

MORSE Right.

ABANES Let that person go on?

MORSE And interestingly enough, there's no debate about that issue in the medical literature. Anyone who has looked at this issue, and many have, they all agree. Article after article has been written saying: Does intensive care medicine do anything?

ABANES Would you advocate this being up to the doctors? Or to the patient? Or to the family?

MORSE I don't really see it that way. Here's what my point is—this might sound like I'm dodging the issue, but I'm not—my point is a simple one: there would be a withering away of the irrational procedures that are rooted in our fear of death. It would be a withering away. It would happen without people even thinking about it. I guess I'm just so convinced that most of these issues are not doctor issues or nurse issues. They're really societal issues.

ABANES Can you define some of those irrational procedures?

MORSE Sure—the use of cardio-pulmonary resuscitation on every dying patient.

ABANES Is there anything you would like to say about this whole euthanasia debate that's going on now with Kevorkian?

MORSE Sure. We wouldn't be having this debate if people really understood about near-death experiences. That we are having such a debate is just a symptom that our society just refuses to talk about death.

ABANES What would you like to see in that area?

MORSE I'd like to see courses on spiritual visions and their significance in death and dying in every medical school and nursing school. I'd like to see, in hospital charts, routine discussion[s] of what the patient's spiritual health is and how that's impacting on what decisions are being made in their treatment.

ABANES What would you like to see if you could have anything you wanted in the way of solving the euthanasia debate, and the problems associated with it?

MORSE The cases that I've seen, that have come down to this kind of dilemma, have all been cases of extremely poor communication in which no one wants to talk about death and dying until the patient is just so frustrated that they say, "Alrighty, I can't get anybody to listen to me. I can't get anybody with any compassion to help me. So, I'll go find a Dr. Kevorkian and kill myself." There shouldn't be this kind of discussion. This should be something between a patient and their family, and their doctor. . . . People just read Betty Eadie's book a few times and they get the idea that it's OK to talk about death. And hopefully when they read it they won't [dwell] on, you know, "It's got too much Mormon imagery in it," and they'll look at sort of the bigger picture that it's trying to say something really important about our human spirit and death. And then, I don't think there would be this problem [euthanasia]. Believe me, there are *many* cases of euthanasia going on *all* the time—and you never hear about it. Patients are allowed to die routinely. Patients are *given* medicines to die routinely. But it's handled in a very personal, a very private way, with a lot of respect and dignity, and everyone knows what's going on. These cases are just symptom[s]. And you can't treat a symptom unless you treat a problem, and the problem is our fear of death and our ignorance about the process of dying.

Bibliography

This is *not* a list of recommended reading. It is a bibliography of sources used while doing research for *Embraced By The Light and the Bible*. The reader should note that many of the following documents are produced by cultic/occultic organizations and contain false doctrines.

Books:

Atwater, P.M.H. *Beyond the Light: What Isn't Being Said About Near-Death Experience.* New York, NY: Carol Publishing Group, 1994.

Barna, George. *The Barna Report: 1992–1993.* Ventura, CA: Regal Books, 1992.

Briggs, Wallace Alvin, ed. *Great Poems of the English Language.* Great Neck, NY: Granger Book Co., Inc., 1982.

Carlson, Richard and Benjamin Shield, eds. *Healers On Healing.* Los Angeles, CA: Jeremy P. Tarcher, Inc., 1989.

Chandler, Russell. *Understanding the New Age.* Grand Rapids, MI: Zondervan Publishing House, 1991.

The Church of Jesus Christ of Latter-day Saints. *Journal of Discourses.* 1966 Edition, Vol. 1. ed. G.D. Watt. London, England: The Church of Jesus Christ of Latter-day Saints (orig. published by F.D. Richards), 1855.

The Church of Jesus Christ of Latter-day Saints. *Journal of*

Discourses. 1966 Edition, Vol. 2. ed. G.D. Watt. London, England: The Church of Jesus Christ of Latter-day Saints (orig. published by F.D. Richards), 1855.

The Church of Jesus Christ of Latter-day Saints. *Journal of Discourses.* 1966 Edition, Vol. 4. ed. G.D. Watt. London, England: The Church of Jesus Christ of Latter-day Saints (orig. published by S.W. Richards), 1857.

The Church of Jesus Christ of Latter-day Saints. *Journal of Discourses.* 1966 Edition, Vol. 6. ed. J.V. Long, G.D. Watt, and Others. London, England: The Church of Jesus Christ of Latter-day Saints (orig. published by Asa Calkin), 1859.

The Church of Jesus Christ of Latter-day Saints. *Journal of Discourses.* 1966 Edition, Vol. 7. ed. J.V. Long, G.D. Watt, and Others. London, England: The Church of Jesus Christ of Latter-day Saints (orig. published by Amasa Lyman), 1860.

The Church of Jesus Christ of Latter-day Saints. *Journal of Discourses.* 1966 Edition, Vol. 8. ed. J.V. Long and G.D. Watt. London, England: The Church of Jesus Christ of Latter-day Saints (orig. published by George Q. Cannon), 1861.

The Church of Jesus Christ of Latter-day Saints. *Journal of Discourses.* 1966 Edition, Vol. 10. ed. G.D. Watt and J.V. Long. London, England: The Church of Jesus Christ of Latter-day Saints (orig. published by Daniel H. Wells), 1865.

The Church of Jesus Christ of Latter-day Saints. *Journal of Discourses.* 1966 Edition, Vol. 11. ed. E.L. Sloan, G.D. Watt, and D.W. Evans. London, England: The Church of Jesus Christ of Latter-day Saints (orig. published by B. Young), 1867.

The Church of Jesus Christ of Latter-day Saints. *Journal of Discourses.* 1966 Edition, Vol. 19. ed. Geo. F. Gibbs, D.W. Evans, and Others. Salt Lake City Utah: The Church of Jesus Christ of Latter-day Saints (orig. published by William Budge), 1878.

The Church of Jesus Christ of Latter-day Saints. *Journal of Discourses.* 1966 Edition, Vol. 26. ed. John Irvine, Geo. F. Gibbs, and Others. London, England: The Church of Jesus Christ of Latter-day Saints (orig. published by Daniel H. Wells), 1886.

The Church of Jesus Christ of Latter-day Saints. *Gospel Principles.* 1979 edition, Salt Lake City, UT: The Church of Jesus Christ of Latter-day Saints, 1978.

Clark, Jerome. *Encyclopedia of Strange and Unexplained Physical Phenomena.* Detroit, MI: Gale Research, Inc., 1993.

Constable, George, ed. *Psychic Voyages.* Mysteries of the Unknown Series editor Pat Daniels. Alexandria, VA: Time-Life Books, 1987.

Creme, Benjamin. *Maitreya's Mission.* London, England: Share International Foundation, 1986.

Creme, Benjamin. *The Reappearance of the Christ and the Masters of Wisdom.* London, England: The Tara Press, 1980.

Deseret News. *Deseret News 1989–1990 Church Almanac.* Salt Lake City, UT: Deseret News, 1988.

Dixon, Jeanne. *Jeanne Dixon: My Life and Prophecies.* New York, NY: William Morrow & Co., 1969.

Dowling, Levi H. *The Aquarian Gospel of Jesus the Christ.* Marina Del Rey, CA: DeVorss & Co., Publishers, 1972.

Drury, Nevill. *Dictionary of Mysticism and the Occult.* First Edition, New York, NY: Harper & Row, 1985.

Eadie, Betty. *Embraced by the Light* (National Edition). Placerville, CA: Gold Leaf Press, 1992.

Eadie, Betty. *Embraced by the Light* (Utah Edition). Placerville, CA: Gold Leaf Press, 1992.

Ehrenborg, Rev. Todd. *Speaking the Truth in Love to the Mind Sciences.* Self-published.

Elwell, Walter A. *Evangelical Dictionary of Theology.* Grand Rapids, MI: Baker Book House, 1984.

Essene, Virginia. *New Teachings for an Awakening Humanity.* Santa Clara, CA: Spiritual Educators Endeavors Publishing Company, 1986.

Ferguson, Marilyn. *The Aquarian Conspiracy.* Los Angeles, CA: J.P. Tarcher, Inc., 1980.

Fodor, Nandor. *An Encyclopedia of Psychic Science.* Second Paperbound Edition, Secaucus, NJ: The Citadel Press, 1966.

Gawain, Shakti. *Living in the Light.* Mill Valley, CA: Whatever Publishing, Inc., 1986.

Geer, Thelma "Granny." *Mormonism, Mamma & Me.* Moody Press 1986 Edition, Chicago, IL: Moody Press, 1979.

Gordon, Henry. *Channeling into the New Age.* Buffalo, NY: Prometheus Books, 1988.

Graham, Billy. *Angels: God's Secret Agents.* Dallas, TX: Word Publishing, 1994.

Groothuis, Douglas R. *Confronting the New Age.* Downers Grove, IL: InterVarsity Press, 1988.

Groothuis, Douglas R. *Revealing the New Age.* Downers Grove, IL: InterVarsity Press, 1990.

Groothuis, Douglas R. *Unmasking the New Age.* Downers Grove, IL: InterVarsity Press, 1986.

Harper Paperbacks. *Funk & Wagnalls Standard Dictionary.* 1983 Edition, New York, NY: Harper Collins Publishers, 1980.

Holroyd, Stuart. *Psychic Voyages*. The Supernatural Series, editor Sally Burningham. London, England: The Danbury Press & Robert B. Clarke, 1976.

Hunter, Milton R. *The Gospel Through the Ages*. Salt Lake City, UT: Deseret Book Company, 1958.

Huxley, Aldous. *The Perennial Philosophy*. First Harper Colophon 1970 Edition, New York, NY: Harper & Row, Inc., 1944.

Ingenito, Marcia Gervase, ed. *National New Age Yellow Pages*. First Edition, Fullerton, CA: The National New Age Yellow Pages, 1987.

Klimo, Jon. *Channeling: Investigations on Receiving Information from Paranormal Sources*. Los Angeles, CA: Jeremy P. Tarcher, Inc., 1987.

Kübler-Ross, Elisabeth. *Death: The Final Stage of Growth*. New York, NY: Simon & Shuster, 1975.

Kübler-Ross, Elisabeth. *On Death and Dying*. New York, NY: Macmillan Publishing Company, 1969.

Lande, Nathaniel. *Mindstyles/Lifestyles*. Los Angeles, CA: Price/Stern/Sloan Publishers, Inc., 1976.

Lutzer, Erwin W. and John F. DeVries. *Satan's "Evangelistic" Strategy for this New Age*. Wheaton, IL: Victor Books, 1989.

Martin, Walter. *The Kingdom of the Cults*. Revised & Expanded April, 1985 Edition, Minneapolis, MN: Bethany House Publishers, 1965.

Martin, Walter. *The Maze of Mormonism*. Revised & Enlarged 1978 Edition, Ventura, CA: Regal Books, 1962.

Martin, Walter. *The New Age Cult*. Minneapolis, MN: Bethany House Publishers, 1989.

McConkie, Bruce. *Mormon Doctrine*. Second Edition (1977), Salt Lake City, UT: Bookcraft, 1966.

McConnell, D.R. *A Different Gospel*. Peabody, MA: Hendrickson Publishers, 1988.

McDowell, Josh. *Handbook of Today's Religions*. San Bernardino, CA: Here's Life Publishers Inc., 1983.

McRoberts, Kerry D. *New Age or Old Lie?*. Peabody, MA: Hendrickson Publishers, Inc., 1989.

Melton, J. Gordon and James R. Lewis, eds. *Perspectives on the New Age*. Albany, NY: State University of New York Press, 1992.

Melton, J. Gordon, Jerome Clark, and Aidan A. Kelly. *New Age Almanac*. Detroit, MI: Gale Research, Inc., 1991.

Melton, J. Gordon, Jerome Clark, and Aidan A. Kelly. *New Age Encyclopedia*. First Edition, Detroit, MI: Gale Research, Inc., 1990.

Melton, J. Gordon. *Encyclopedia of American Religions*. Fourth Edition, Detroit, MI: Gale Research, Inc., 1993.

Miller, Elliot. *A Crash Course on the New Age*. Grand Rapids, MI: Baker Book House, 1989.

Moody, Raymond A. *Life After Life*. New York, NY: Bantam, 1975.

Moody, Raymond A. *The Light Beyond*. New York, NY: Bantam, 1988.

The Norton Company. *The Norton Anthology of Poetry*. 1983 Edition, New York, NY: W.W. Norton & Company, 1970.

Peretti, Frank E. *This Present Darkness*. Westchester, IL: Crossway Books, 1986.

Peters, Ted. *The Cosmic Self*. San Francisco, CA: Harper San Francisco, 1991.

Pfeiffer, Charles F. and Everett F. Harrison, eds. *The Wycliffe Bible Commentary*. Chicago: Moody Press, 1990.

"Ramtha" With Douglas James Mahr. *Voyage to the New World*. Friday Harbor, WA: Masterworks, Inc., 1985.

Rawlings, Dr. Maurice. *To Hell and Back*. Nashville, TN: Thomas Nelson Publishers, 1993.

Reisser, Paul C., Teri K. Reisser, and John Weldon. *New Age Medicine*. Downers Grove, IL: InterVarsity Press, 1987.

Rhodes, Ron. *The Counterfeit Christ of the New Age Movement*. Grand Rapids, MI: Baker Book House, 1990.

Rhodes, Ron. *The Culting of America*. Eugene, OR: Harvest House, 1994.

Richards, Le Grand. *A Marvelous Work and A Wonder*. Salt Lake City, UT: Deseret Book Company, 1950.

Ring, Kenneth. *Heading Toward Omega: In Search of the Meaning of the Near-Death Experience*. New York, NY: William Morrow & Co., Inc., 1984.

Ring, Kenneth. *Life At Death: A Scientific Investigation of the Near-Death Experience*. New York, NY: Coward McCann & Geoghegan, 1980.

Ring, Kenneth. *The Omega Project: Near-Death Experiences, UFO Encounters, and Mind at Large*. New York, NY: William Morrow & Co., Inc., 1992.

Roberts, B.H. *Mormon Doctrine of Deity*. Reprint Edition, Bountiful, UT: Horizon Publishers, 1903.

Rudolf Steiner Publications. *The Steinerbooks Dictionary of the Psychic, Mystic, Occult*. Blauvelt, NY: Rudolf Steiner Publications, 1973.

Sabom, Dr. Michael B. *Recollections of Death: A Medical Investigation*. New York, NY: Harper & Row, 1982.

Samples, Kenneth, Erwin deCastro, Richard Abanes, and Robert Lyle. *Prophets of the Apocalypse: David Koresh and Other American Messiahs*. Grand Rapids, MI: Baker Book House, 1994.

Shepard, Leslie A., ed. *Encyclopedia of Occultism & Parapsychology*. Second Edition, Vol. 1. Detroit, MI: Gale Research Company, 1984.

Shepard, Leslie A., ed. *Encyclopedia of Occultism & Parapsychology*. Second Edition, Vol. 2. Detroit, MI: Gale Research Company, 1984.

Shepard, Leslie A., ed. *Encyclopedia of Occultism & Parapsychology*. Second Edition, Vol. 3. Detroit, MI: Gale Research Company, 1985.

Smith Jr., Joseph. *Book of Mormon*. 1981 edition, Salt Lake City, UT: The Church of Jesus Christ of Latter-day Saints, 1830.

Smith Jr., Joseph. *Doctrine & Covenants*. 1981 edition, Salt Lake City, UT: The Church of Jesus Christ of Latter-day Saints, 1835.

Smith Jr., Joseph. *Pearl of Great Price*. 1981 edition, Salt Lake City, UT: The Church of Jesus Christ of Latter-day Saints, 1851.

Smith, Joseph Fielding, ed. *Teachings of the Prophet Joseph Smith*. Salt Lake City, UT: Deseret Book Company, 1976.

Smith, Joseph Fielding. *Doctrines of Salvation*. Vol. 1., Salt Lake City, UT: Bookcraft, 1954.

Smith, Joseph Fielding. *The Way to Perfection*. Salt Lake City, UT: Genealogical Society of Utah, 1931.

Sneed, Dr. David and Dr. Sharon Sneed. *The Hidden Agenda*. Nashville, TN: Thomas Nelson Publishers, Inc., 1991.

Spangler, David. *Revelation: The Birth of a New Age*. San Francisco, CA: The Rainbow Bridge, 1976.

Stemman, Roy. *Spirits and Spirit Worlds*. The Supernatural Series, editor Eleanor Van Zandt. London, England: The Danbury Press & Robert B. Clarke, 1975.

Talmage, James E. *A Study of the Articles of Faith*. Salt Lake City, UT: The Church of Jesus Christ of Latter-day Saints, 1948.

Tolbert, Keith and Eric Pement. *The 1993 Directory of Cult Research Organizations*. 1993 Edition, Trenton, MI: American Religions Center, 1993.

Tondriau, Julien. *The Occult: Secrets of the Hidden World* (originally published in France as *L'occultisme*). Pyramid Communications, Inc. 1972 Edition, translated by Bay Bocks Pty. Ltd. Verviers, France: Editions Gerard & Co., 1964.

Two Disciples. *The Rainbow Bridge*. Second 1982 Edition, Escondido, CA: The Triune Foundation, 1981.

Valiente, Doreen. *An ABC of Witchcraft*. New York, NY: St. Martin's Press, Inc., 1973.

Van Wagoner, Richard S. and Steven C. Walker. *A Book of Mormon*. Salt Lake City, UT: Signature Books, 1982.

Vincent, Ken R. *Visions of God*. Burdett, NY: Larson Publications, 1994.

Weldon, John and Clifford Wilson. *Psychic Forces and Occult Shock*. Chattanooga, TN: Global Publishers, 1987.

Winkler, Eldon K. *The New Age Is Lying to You.* St. Louis, MO: Concordia Publishing House, 1994.

Zaleski, Carol. *Otherworld Journeys: Accounts of Near-Death Experience in Medieval and Modern Times.* New York, NY: Oxford University Press, 1987.

Newspapers, Magazines and Journals

Abanes, Richard and Paul Carden. "A Special Report: What is Betty Eadie Hiding?" *Christian Research Journal* 16:3 (Winter 1994), pp. 6, 40–41.

Abanes, Richard. "Readers Embrace the Light." *Christianity Today,* 3/7/94, p. 53.

Albrecht, Mark and Brooks Alexander. "Thanatology: Death and Dying," *Journal of the Spiritual Counterfeits Project,* April 1977, pp. 5–11.

Associated Press. "Reports of Near-Death Experiences Grow: Causes Still A Mystery." *The Atlanta Journal and Constitution,* 6/25/89, p. A11.

Benanti, Joseph A. and Jeffrey J. Ellis. " 'The New Age: An Old Lie,' A Christian Perspective on the New Age Movement." Newsletter, pp. 1, 4–5. Port Gibson, NY: National Association of Christian Physical Therapists, 1989.

Benanti, Joseph A. and Jeffrey J. Ellis. "A Christian Perspective on the New Age Movement Bio-Energy: The 'Current Trend.' " Newsletter, pp. 1, 3–6. Port Gibson, NY: National Association of Christian Physical Therapists, 1989.

Benanti, Joseph A. and Jeffrey J. Ellis. "A Christian Perspective on the New Age Movement—Altered Consciousness:

Gateway to Self-Realization or Self-Destruction." Newsletter, pp. 1, 4-8. Port Gibson, NY: National Association of Christian Physical Therapists, 1989-1990.

Benanti, Joseph A. and Jeffrey J. Ellis. "Christian Perspective on the New Age Movement—Confronting or Converting." Newsletter, pp. 1, 3–7. Port Gibson, NY: National Association of Christian Physical Therapists, 1990.

Boren, Karen. "Is Death Merely the Precipice of True Birth?" *Deseret News*, 1/17/93, n.p.

Bush, Nancy Evans. "We Appreciate Your Asking About Near-Death Experiences and IANDS." Publicity Letter to Constituents, International Association for Near-Death Studies (IANDS).

Cox, Meg. "Death Conquers Bestseller Lists as Boomers Age." *Wall Street Journal*, 2/23/94, pp. B1, B18.

Dart, John. "After 'Near-Death,' Atheist Yields Slightly on Afterlife." *Los Angeles Times*, 10/8/88, p. 2 (section II).

DeCastro, Erwin, B.J. Oropeza, and Ron Rhodes. "Enter the Dragon? Wrestling with the Martial Arts Phenomenon (part 1)." *Christian Research Journal* 16:2 (Fall 1993), pp. 26–34.

Deseret Books. *IMPRESSIONS* 4:3. Salt Lake City, UT: Deseret Books, 1994, pp. 3, 5.

Detjen, Jim. "Near-Death Experience Changes Lives." *Tallahassee Democrat*, 1/8/89, pp. 1G, 10G.

Ebert, Alan. "A Glimpse of Heaven." *Redbook*, July 1991, pp. 88–89, 128.

Eddington, Mark. "Eadie's Appearance Ties Up Traffic." *Davis County Clipper*, 2/12/93, p. 2.

Ford, Marcia. "Mormon Book Lures Christians." *Charisma & Christian Life*, July 1994, p. 64.

Genova, Amy Sunshine. "The Near-Death Experience." *McCall's*, February 1988, pp. 102, 104–106.

Gold Leaf Press. "Embraced by the Light: National Media Tour." Publicity Material, Placerville, CA: Gold Leaf Press, 1994.

Gold Leaf Press. "What Is It Like to Die? Betty Eadie Knows." Publicity Material, Placerville, CA: Gold Leaf Press, 1994.

Haas, Jane Glenn. " 'The Light': Doctor Explores People's Near-Death Experiences." *Orange County Register*, 10/21/92, p. E3.

Haas, Jane Glenn. "Into the Light." *The Orange County Register*, 1/10/93, pp. 1–2 (Accent Section).

Ho, Vanessa. "Brush with Death Puts Her in the Publishing Spotlight." *Seattle Times*, 6/27/93, p. L3.

Holt, Dennis R. "Letters." *Charisma & Christian Life*, 1994.

Jerome, Jim. "Heaven Can Wait." PEOPLE, 10/11/93, pp. 81–83.

Jones, Verna Noel. "Closer to Light: Kids Share Near-Death Experiences." *Rocky Mountain News*, 10/14/90, pp. 20M–21M.

Kee, Christine A. and Nancy Pridmore. "Near-Death Experiences: An Interview with Kenneth Ring." *Plato's Cave* (Philosophy Circular), pp. 1–4. Walnut, CA: Mount San Antonio College, 1991.

Krier, Beth Ann. "Near-Death Visions." *Los Angeles Times*, 9/18/90, pp. E1, E6, E7.

Larson, Viola. "Identity: A 'Christian' Religion for White Racists." *Christian Research Journal* 15:2 (Fall 1992), pp. 21–28.

Longley, Ann. "A Glimpse Beyond." *PEOPLE*, 8/1/94, pp. 43–44.

Lueders, Beth. "Out of Body or Out of Your Mind." *Clarity*, May/June 1994, pp. 27–32.

Mauro, James. "Bright Lights, Big Mystery." *Psychology Today*, July/August 1992, pp. 54–57, 80–82.

McClain, Rhonda. "A Brush With Death: Heaven's Gate." *The Morning News Tribune*, 10/27/91, pp. 3–4, 7 (section F).

Miller, Elliot. "The Christian, Energetic Medicine, and 'New Age Paranoia.' " *Christian Research Journal* 14:3 (Winter 1992), pp. 24–27.

Miller, Leslie. "Betty Eadie, Shedding 'Light' on Her Visit to Heaven." *USA Today*, 8/12/93, p. 5D.

n.a. "*Embraced by the Light* Author Is Mormon." *Bookstore Journal* December 1993, p. 14.

n.a. "GOLD LEAF PRESS" (advertisement). *Publisher's Weekly*, August 8, 1994, p. 189.

n.a. "IANDS." *Publicity Brochure*. East Windsor Hill, CT: International Association for Near-Death Studies.

n.a. "Imagine A World of Possibilities." *1994 Whole Life Expo Program Guide*. San Francisco, CA: Whole Life Expo Staff, 1994.

n.a. "Near-Death Best Seller Sparks Questions." *Bookstore Journal*, November 1993, p. 26.

n.a. "Near-Death of 7-year-old Reported." *American Medical News*, 10/21/83, p. 42.

n.a. "The Near-Death Experience—How Thousands Describe It." *U.S. News & World Report*, June 11, 1984, pp. 59–60.

n.a. "The Plowboy Interview: Elisabeth Kübler–Ross on Living, Dying . . . and Beyond." *The Mother Earth News*, May/June 1983, pp. 17–22.

Nietzke, Ann. "The Miracle of Kübler-Ross." *Human Behavior* (1977) as reprinted in *Cosmopolitan*, February 1980, pp. 206–211, 254.

Pearson, Mike. "Into the Light: Near-Death Experiences." *Rocky Mountain News*, 3/15/89, pp. 48–49.

Perlah, Jeffrey L. "People in Books: An Amazing First-Time Success Story." *American Bookseller*, June 1993, p. 64.

Perry, Paul. "Brushes with Death." *Psychology Today*, September 1988, pp. 14–15.

Philips, Valerie. "Author Shares Love of Life After Death in an Embrace." *Standard-Examiner*, 3/6/93, n.p.

Porvaznik, Philip J. "Near Death or Deception?: An Analysis of the NDE from a Biblical Perspective." Unpublished Manuscript. University of South Florida, n.d.

Price, Kathie. "Visiting Death: Woman Tells of Glimpse of Paradise." *The Arizona Republic*, 3/13/93, pp. B6–B7.

Rosenbaum, Ron. "Turn On, Tune In, Drop Dead." *HARPER'S*, July 1982, pp. 32–42.

Santmire, H. Paul. "Nothing More Beautiful Than Death?" The Christian Century, 12/14/83, pp. 1154–1158.

Somerville, Barbara. "Brushes with Death Cast New Light on Life." *Denver Post*, 5/13/90, pp. 10, 23.

Stack, Peggy Fletcher. "Mormon's Book on Afterlife Gains National Response." *Salt Lake Tribune*, 10/23/93, p. D2.

Stuart, Janis. "'Embraced' Author Nearly Squeezed Out of Auditorium." *Davis County Clipper*, 2/12/93, p. 2.

Swenson, Paul. "Embraced by the Light." *Salt Lake Tribune*, 12/20/92, p. PE11.

Underwood, Nora. "Between Life and Death." *MACLEAN'S*, 4/20/92, pp. 34–38.

Viotti, Vicki. " 'Embraced By The Light' Author Puts Accent on Afterlife." *The Honolulu Advertiser*, 6/13/94, pp. B1–B4.

Wallis, Claudia. "Going Gentle into That Good Night." *TIME*, 2/8/92, pp. 79.

White, John. "Beyond the Body: An Examination of the Near-Death Experience—An Interview with Kenneth Ring." *Science of Mind*, November 1982, pp. 8–15, 84–90.

Witherrite, Jacquie and Shirlee Teabo. "Little Bit of Heaven May Be Locked in Our Brains." *The Morning News Tribune*, 12/8/91, n.p.

Witherrite, Jacquie and Shirlee Teabo. "Medical Professionals Gain Knowledge of Afterlife, Past Lives." *The Morning News Tribune*, 7/26/92, pp. 6–7.

Yamamoto, J. Isamu. "The Near-Death Experience (part 1)." *Christian Research Journal* 14:4 (Spring 1992), pp. 21–23, 30–32.

Yamamoto, J. Isamu. "The Near-Death Experience (part 2)." *Christian Research Journal* 15:1 (Summer 1992), pp. 15–19, 29.

Recorded Interviews

Baer, Dick: 1/25/94.

Brawner, Lonnette: 7/26/94.

Bush, Nancy Evans: 8/1/94.

Eadie, Betty: 1/25/94.

Kittel, Bill: 8/4/94.

Morse, Dr. Melvin: 7/29/94.

Ring, Dr. Kenneth: 7/22/94.

Sabom, Dr. Michael: 8/3/94.

Non-Recorded Interviews

Miller, Dan (LDS Bishop of Seattle, Washington's Ninth Ward): 1/21/94.

Fitzgerald, Nephi (Aspen Books Employee): 6/28/94.

IANDS (International Association for Near-Death Studies): 7/20/94.

Miscellaneous Sources

"20/20" program (ABC): 5/13/94.

"The Oprah Winfrey Show" (ABC): 1/3/94 & 8/3/94.

"Leeza" (NBC): 6/13/94

"American Journal" (Syndicated): 2/94.

"Talk From the Heart" with Al Kresta (WMUZ): 3/3/94.